The Road to Serfdom

with The Intellectuals and Socialism

The Road to Serfdom

with The Intellectuals and Socialism

FRIEDRICH A. HAYEK

THE CONDENSED VERSION OF *THE ROAD TO SERFDOM* BY F. A. HAYEK AS IT APPEARED IN THE APRIL 1945 EDITION OF *READER'S DIGEST*

The Institute of Economic Affairs

This combined edition first published in Great Britain in 2005 by
The Institute of Economic Affairs
2 Lord North Street
Westminster
London SW1P 3LB
in association with Profile Books Ltd

This condensed version of *The Road to Serfdom* was first published in Great Britain in 1999
in the 'Rediscovered Riches' series by The Institute of Economic Affairs, and reissued as
Occasional Paper 122 in 2001

This condensed version of *The Road to Serfdom* © *Reader's Digest*,
reproduced by kind permission

The Road to Serfdom is published in all territories outside the USA by Routledge.
This version is published by kind permission.

'The Intellectuals and Socialism' previously published in Great Britain in 1998 in the
'Rediscovered Riches' series by the Institute of Economic Affairs

'The Intellectuals and Socialism' © The University of Chicago Law Review 1949.
Reproduced by kind permission.

All other material copyright © The Institute of Economic Affairs 2005

The mission of the Institute of Economic Affairs is to improve public understanding of
the fundamental institutions of a free society, with particular reference to the role of
markets in solving economic and social problems.

A CIP catalogue record for this book is available from the British Library.

ISBN 0 255 36576 4

Many IEA publications are translated into languages other than English or are reprinted.
Permission to translate or to reprint should be sought from the Director General at the
address above.

Typeset in Stone by MacGuru
info@macguru.org.uk
Printed and bound in Great Britain by Hobbs the Printers

CONTENTS

THE AUTHORS

Friedrich A. Hayek

Friedrich A. Hayek (1899–1992) was born in Vienna and obtained two doctorates from the University of Vienna, in law and political economy. He worked under Ludwig von Mises at the Austrian Institute for Business Cycle Research, and from 1929 to 1931 was a lecturer in economics at the University of Vienna. His first book, *Monetary Theory and the Trade Cycle*, was published in 1929. In 1931 Hayek was made Tooke Professor of Economic Science and Statistics at the London School of Economics, and in 1950 he was appointed Professor of Social and Moral Sciences at the University of Chicago. In 1962 he was appointed Professor of Political Economy at the University of Freiburg, where he became Professor Emeritus in 1967. Hayek was elected a Fellow of the British Academy in 1944, and in 1947 he organised the conference in Switzerland which resulted in the creation of the Mont Pèlerin Society. He was awarded the Nobel Prize in Economics in 1974 and was created a Companion of Honour in 1984. In 1991 George Bush awarded Hayek the Presidential Medal of Freedom. His books include *The Pure Theory of Capital*, 1941, *The Road to Serfdom*, 1944, *The Counter-Revolution of Science*, 1952, *The Constitution of Liberty*, 1960, *Law, Legislation and Liberty*, 1973–9, and *The Fatal Conceit*, 1988.

John Blundell

John Blundell is Director General of the Institute of Economic Affairs. He was previously President of the Institute for Humane Studies at George Mason University and the Atlas Economic Research Foundation, founded by the late Sir Antony Fisher to establish 'sister' organisations to the IEA. He serves on the boards of both organisations and is a former Vice President of the Mont Pèlerin Society.

Edwin J. Feulner Jr

Edwin J. Feulner Jr has served as President of the Heritage Foundation since 1977. He is a past President of the Mont Pèlerin Society. He previously served in high-level positions in both the legislative and executive branches of the United States federal government. He received his Ph.D. from the University of Edinburgh and was awarded the Presidential Citizen's Medal by Ronald Reagan in 1989 for 'being a leader of the conservative movement by building an organisation dedicated to ideas and their consequences . . .'

Walter E. Williams

Walter Williams is John M. Olin Distinguished Professor of Economics at George Mason University, Fairfax, Virginia. In addition, he serves as an Adjunct Professor of Economics at Grove City College in Grove City, Pennsylvania. He has also served on the faculties of Los Angeles City College, California State University Los Angeles, and Temple University in Philadelphia. He is the author of over eighty publications that have appeared in scholarly journals such as *Economic Inquiry*, *American Economic Review*,

Georgia Law Review, Journal of Labor Economics and *Social Science Quarterly*, as well as popular publications such as *Newsweek, The Freeman, National Review, Reader's Digest, Cato Journal* and *Policy Review*. Dr Williams serves on the boards of directors of Citizens for a Sound Economy, the Reason Foundation and the Hoover Institution, and on the advisory boards of the IEA, the Landmark Legal Foundation, the Alexis de Tocqueville Institute, the Cato Institute and others. He has frequently given expert testimony before Congressional committees on public policy issues ranging from labour policy to taxation and spending. He is a member of the Mont Pèlerin Society and the American Economic Association.

FOREWORD

Friedrich A. Hayek was one of the twentieth century's greatest philosophers. While he is best known for his work in economics, he also made significant contributions in political philosophy and law. The publication for which Professor Hayek is most widely known is *The Road to Serfdom*, written during World War II, the condensed *Reader's Digest* version of which is presented here along with what might be seen as his follow-up, *The Intellectuals and Socialism*, first published by the *University of Chicago Law Review* in 1949.

A focal point of *The Road to Serfdom* was to offer an explanation for the rise of Nazism, to correct the popular and erroneous view that it was caused by a character defect of the German people. Hayek differs, saying that the horrors of Nazism would have been inconceivable among the German people a mere fifteen years before Adolf Hitler's rise to power. Indeed, 'throughout most of its history [Germany was] one of the most tolerant European countries for Jews'.[1] Other evidence against the character defect argument is that the writings of some German philosophers, such as Johann Wolfgang von Goethe, Wilhelm von Humboldt and Friedrich Schiller, served as inspiration for ideas about the liberal

---

1   Thomas Sowell, *The Economics and Politics of Race*, William Morrow & Company, New York, 1983, p. 86.

order later expressed in the writings of British philosophers such as John Stuart Mill and David Hume.

What happened in Germany? Hayek explains, 'The supreme tragedy is still not seen that in Germany it was largely people of good will who, by their socialist policies, prepared the way for forces which stand for everything they detest'. Hayek's explanation for the rise of Nazism was not understood and appreciated in 1944, and it is still not fully understood and appreciated today. Collectivism, whether it is in Germany, the former Soviet Union, Britain or the USA, makes personal liberty its victim.

How do we combat collectivism? Hayek provides some answers in *The Intellectuals and Socialism*. In a word or two, those who support the liberal social order must attack the intellectual foundations of collectivism. Hayek urges that an understanding of just what it is that leads many intellectuals toward socialism is vital. It is neither, according to Hayek, selfish interests nor evil intentions that motivate intellectuals towards socialism. On the contrary, they are motivated by 'mostly honest convictions and good intentions'. Hayek adds that it is necessary to recognise that 'the typical intellectual is today more likely to be a socialist the more he is guided by good will and intelligence'. Joseph A. Schumpeter differed, seeing Hayek's assessment as 'politeness to a fault'.[2]

Hayek argues that the roots of collectivism have nowhere originated among working-class people. Its roots lie among intellectuals – the people Hayek refers to as 'second-hand dealers in ideas' – who had to work long and hard to get working-class people to

---

2   J. Schumpeter, review of *The Road to Serfdom*, *Journal of Political Economy*, June 1946: 269–270.

accept the vision they put forward. The intellectuals or second-hand dealers in ideas to whom he refers are journalists, teachers, ministers, radio commentators, cartoonists and artists, who Hayek says 'are masters of the technique of conveying ideas but are usually amateurs so far as the substance of what they convey is concerned'.

In 1949, when Hayek wrote *The Intellectuals and Socialism*, the second-hand dealers in collectivist ideas were a dominant force. He appeared to be pessimistic about the future of liberty because those who were on the conservative/free market side of the political spectrum were weak, isolated and had little voice. In 1947, Hayek, along with several other distinguished free market scholars, addressed some of the isolation by founding the Mont Pèlerin Society. The purpose of the Society was to hold meetings and present papers and exchange ideas among like-minded scholars with the hope of strengthening the principles of a free society. The Mont Pèlerin Society now has over 500 members worldwide, and can boast that eight of its members have won Nobel Prizes in economics.

Since Hayek wrote *The Intellectuals and Socialism* there has been nothing less than monumental change in the marketplace of ideas. In 1949, there was only one free market organisation – The Foundation for Economic Education, founded by Leonard Read. Today there are over 350 free market organisations in 50 countries, including former communist countries. The major media no longer has the monopoly on news and the dissemination of ideas that it once had. Network television faces competition from satellite and cable television. Talk radio has exploded. *The Rush Limbaugh Show*, on which I have served as occasional substitute host for over thirteen years, is carried on 625 different radio stations, on satellite and over the internet, reaching tens of millions of people worldwide each week. Much to socialist dismay, the most popular and successful talk radio shows are those hosted by conservative/free market hosts. Then there are the bloggers – the electronic equivalent of conservative/free market journalists – who are constantly at the ready to challenge and reveal news stories.

While there have been monumental changes in the ideas marketplace, the last bastion of solidly entrenched socialism lies on college and university campuses around the world. Hayek argues that 'It is perhaps the most characteristic feature of the intellectual that he judges new ideas not by their specific merits but by the readiness with which they fit into his general conceptions, into the picture of the world which he regards as modern or advanced'.

Professor Thomas Sowell puts the argument in another way that encompasses Hayek's.[3] Sowell says that there are essentially two visions of how the world operates – the constrained vision and the unconstrained. The constrained vision sees mankind with its moral limitations, acquisitiveness and ego as inherent and immutable. Under this vision, the fundamental challenge that confronts mankind is to organise a system consisting of social mores, customs and laws that make the best of the human condition rather than waste resources trying to change human nature. It is this constrained vision of mankind that underlies the thinking and writings of Adam Smith, Edmund Burke and Alexander Hamilton, among others.

---

3   Thomas Sowell, *A Conflict of Visions: Ideological Origins of Political Struggles*, William Morrow & Company, New York, 1987.

By contrast, the unconstrained vision sees mankind as capable of perfection and capable of putting the interests of others first. Sowell says that no other eighteenth-century writer's vision stands in starker contrast to that of Adam Smith than William Godwin's in *Enquiry Concerning Political Justice*. Godwin viewed *intention* to benefit others as the essence of virtue that leads to human happiness. Benefits to others that arise unintentionally are virtually worthless. Sowell says, 'Unlike Smith, who regarded human selfishness as a given, Godwin regarded it as being promoted by the very system of rewards used to cope with it'.[4]

In the last paragraph of *The Intellectuals and Socialism*, Hayek says, 'Unless we [true liberals] can make the philosophic foundation of a free society once more a living intellectual issue, ... the prospects of freedom are indeed dark'. If Hayek is correct that neither selfish interests nor evil intentions motivate intellectuals towards socialism, there are indeed grounds for optimism. Education offers hope. We can educate them, or at least make others immune, to the errors of their thinking.

I think the strategy has at least two principal components. First, there is not a lot to be gained by challenging the internal logic of many socialist arguments. Instead, it is the initial premises that underlie their arguments that must be challenged. Take one small example. One group of people articulates a concern for the low-skilled worker and argues for an increase in the minimum wage as a means to help them. Another group of people articulating the identical concern might just as strongly oppose an increase in the minimum wage, arguing that it will hurt low-skilled workers.

How can people who articulate identical ends, as is so often

---

4   Ibid., p. 24.

the case, strongly defend polar opposite policies? I believe part of the answer is that they make different initial premises of how the world works. If one's initial premise is that an employer needs so many workers to perform a particular job, then enacting a higher minimum wage means that all the workers will keep their jobs. The only difference is that they will receive higher wages and the employer will make less profit. Thus, enacting a higher minimum wage clearly benefits low-skilled workers. By contrast, if one's initial premise is that there are alternative means to produce a product, and employers will seek the least-cost method of doing so, then raising the minimum wage will cause employers to seek substitutes such as automation or relocation overseas, thereby reducing the amount of workers they hire. With the latter vision, one can have the interests of low-skilled workers at heart and oppose an increase in the minimum wage, because it reduces opportunities for low-skilled workers. If Hayek is correct in his assessment of socialists, it would appear that it is a simple task to empirically show that there are alternative methods of production and that employers are not insensitive to increases in the cost of workers.

The second part of the strategy is to make better, unassailable arguments for personal liberty. Any part of the socialist agenda can be shown as immoral under the assumption that people own themselves. The idea of self ownership makes certain forms of behaviour unambiguously immoral. Murder, rape and theft are immoral simply because they violate a person's property rights to himself. Government programmes such as subsidies to farmers, bailouts for businesses, and welfare or medical care for the indigent are also immoral for the same reason. Government has no resources of its very own. The only way government can give one person money is to first take it from another person. Doing so represents the forcible using of one person, through the tax code, to serve the purposes of another. That is a form of immorality akin to slavery. After all, a working definition of slavery is precisely that: the forcible use of one person to serve the purposes of another.

Well-intentioned socialists, if they are honest people as Hayek contends, should be able to appreciate that reaching into one's own pockets to assist one's fellow man is laudable and praiseworthy. Reaching into another's pocket to do so is theft and by any standard of morality should be condemned.

Collectivists can neither ignore nor dismiss irrefutable evidence that free markets produce unprecedented wealth. Instead, they indict the free market system on moral grounds, charging that it is a system that rewards greed and selfishness and creates an unequal distribution of income. Free markets must be defended on moral grounds. We must convince our fellow man there cannot be personal liberty in the absence of free markets, respect for private property rights and rule of law. Even if free markets were not superior wealth producers, the morality of the market would make them the superior alternative.

WALTER E. WILLIAMS
John M. Olin Distinguished Professor of Economics
George Mason University, Fairfax, Virginia
May 2005

The views expressed in Occasional Paper 136 are, as in all IEA publications, those of the author and not those of the Institute (which has no corporate view), its managing trustees, Academic Advisory Council members or senior staff.

The Road to Serfdom

FOREWORD

John Chamberlain characterised the period immediately following World War II in his foreword to the first edition of *The Road to Serfdom* as 'a time of hesitation'. Britain and the European continent were faced with the daunting task of reconstruction and reconstitution. The United States, spared from the physical destruction that marked Western Europe, was nevertheless recovering from the economic whiplash of a war-driven economic recovery from the Great Depression. Everywhere there was a desire for security and a return to stability.

The intellectual environment was no more steady. The rise and subsequent defeat of fascism had provided an extremely wide flank for intellectuals who were free to battle for any idea short of ethnic cleansing and dictatorial political control. At the same time, the mistaken but widely accepted notion that the unpredictability of the free market had caused the depression, coupled with four years of war-driven, centrally directed production, and the fact that Russia had been a wartime ally of the United States and England, increased the mainstream acceptance of peace-time government planning of the economy.

At this hesitating, unstable moment appeared the slim volume of which you now hold the condensed version in your hands, F. A. Hayek's *The Road to Serfdom*. Occupying his spare time between September 1940 and March 1944, the writing of *The Road to Serfdom* was in his own words more 'a duty which I must not evade'[1] than any calculated contribution to his curriculum vitae. As Hayek saw it, he was merely pointing out 'apprehensions which current tendencies [in economic and political thought] must create in the minds of many who cannot publicly express them . . .'[2] But as is often the case, this duty-inspired task had tremendous consequences unintended by the author.

Hayek employed economics to investigate the mind of man, using the knowledge he had gained to unveil the totalitarian nature of socialism and to explain how it inevitably leads to 'serfdom'. His greatest contribution lay in the discovery of a simple yet profound truth: man does not and cannot know everything, and when he acts as if he does, disaster follows. He recognised that socialism, the collectivist state, and planned economies represent the ultimate form of *hubris*, for those who plan them attempt – with insufficient knowledge – to redesign the nature of man. In so doing, would-be planners arrogantly ignore traditions that embody the wisdom of generations; impetuously disregard customs whose purpose they do not understand; and blithely confuse the law written on the hearts of men – which they cannot change – with administrative rules that they can alter at whim. For Hayek, such presumption was not only a 'fatal conceit', but also 'the road to serfdom'.

The impact of the simple ideas encapsulated in *The Road to Serfdom* was immediate. The book went through six impressions in the first 16 months, was translated into numerous foreign languages, and circulated both openly in the free world and clan-

1   F. A. Hayek, *The Road to Serfdom,* Routledge, London, 1944, p. v.
2   Ibid., p. vii.

destinely behind the emerging iron curtain. It is no exaggeration to say that *The Road to Serfdom* simultaneously prevented the emergence of full-blown socialism in Western Europe and the United States and planted seeds of freedom in the Soviet Union that would finally bear fruit nearly 45 years later. Socialist catch-phrases such as 'collectivism' were stricken from the mainstream political debate and even academic socialists were forced to retreat from their defence of overt social planning.

But the true value of *The Road to Serfdom* is to be found not in the immediate blow it dealt to socialist activists and thinkers – as important as that was – but in the lasting impression it has made on political and economic thinkers of the past 55 years. By Hayek's own admission, 'this book ... has unexpectedly become for me the starting point of more than 30 years' work in a new field'.[3]

EDWIN J. FEULNER JR

November 1999

---

3 Although these words were written in 1976 it is safe to say that the influence of *The Road to Serfdom* guided Hayek's work until his death in 1992.

INTRODUCTION

HAYEK, FISHER AND
THE ROAD TO SERFDOM[1]

My story begins with a young Englishman named Lionel Robbins, later Lord Robbins of Clare Market. In 1929, at the age of only 30, he had been appointed Professor of Economics at the London School of Economics and Political Science (LSE), a college of the University of London. He was arguably the greatest English economist of his generation, and he was fluent in German. This skill alerted him to the work of a young Austrian economist, Friedrich Hayek, and he invited his equally young counterpart to lecture at the LSE. Such was the success of these lectures that Hayek was appointed Tooke Professor of Economic Science and Statistics at the LSE in 1931, and became an English citizen long before such status had become a 'passport of convenience'.

In the 1930s John Maynard Keynes was in full flow. He was the most famous economist in the world, and Hayek was his only real rival. In 1936 Keynes published his infamous *General Theory of Employment, Interest and Money*.[2] Hayek was tempted to demolish this nonsense but he held back, for a very simple and very human reason. Two years earlier, a now forgotten Keynesian tract (*A*

---

1   This introduction is based on a speech given by the author on 26 April 1999 to the 33rd International Workshop 'Books for a Free Society' of the Atlas Economic Research Foundation (Fairfax, VA) in Philadelphia, PA.

2   J. M. Keynes, *The General Theory of Employment, Interest and Money*, Macmillan, London, 1936.

Treatise on Money)[3] had been ripped apart by Hayek in a two-part journal review. Keynes had shrugged off the attack with a smile, saying as they passed one day in Clare Market: 'Oh, never mind; I no longer believe all that.' Hayek was not about to repeat the demolition job on *The General Theory* in case Keynes decided, at some future point, that he no longer believed in 'all that' either – a decision I heard Hayek regret often in the 1970s.

War came and the LSE was evacuated from central London to Peterhouse College, Cambridge. Typically, Keynes arranged rooms for his intellectual arch-rival Hayek at King's College where Keynes was Bursar and – also typically – Hayek volunteered for fire duty. That is, he offered to spend his nights sitting on the roof of his college watching out for marauding German bombers.

It was while he sat out there at night that he began to wonder about what would happen to his adopted country if and when peace came. It was clear to Hayek that victory held the seeds of its own destruction. The war was called 'the People's War' because – unlike most previous wars – the whole population had fought in one way or another. Even pacifists contributed by working the land to feed the troops. Hayek detected a growing sense of 'As in war, so in peace' – namely that the government would own, plan and control everything. The economic difficulties created by the war would be immense: people would turn to government for a way out. And so, as Hayek penned his great classic, *The Road to Serfdom*, he was moved not only by a love for his adopted country but also by a great fear that national planning, that socialism, that the growth of state power and control would, inevitably, lead the UK and the US to fascism, or rather National Socialism.

---

3   J. M. Keynes, A *Treatise on Money*, Macmillan, London, 1930.

Antony Fisher, the man who did

So let me talk now about *The Road to Serfdom* and one man in particular who was moved by its lessons to do something. That man is the late Antony George Anson Fisher, or AGAF as we referred to him, and still do.

Fisher came from a family of mine owners, members of parliament, migrants and military men. He was born in 1915 and soon followed by his brother and best friend Basil. His father was killed by a Turkish sniper in 1917. Brought up in South East England by his young widowed mother, an independent New Zealander from Piraki, Akaroa, AGAF attended Eton and Cambridge, where he and his brother both learnt to fly in the University Air Squadron. On graduating, Antony's several initiatives included:

- a car rental firm – a success
- a plane rental firm – also a success; and
- the design and manufacture of a cheap sports car called the Deroy – a failure because of a lack of power.

At the start of the war Antony and Basil volunteered for the RAF and were soon flying Hurricanes in III Squadron in the Battle of Britain. One day Basil's plane was hit by German fire. He bailed out over Selsey Bill but his parachute was on fire and both plane and man plummeted to the ground, separately.

A totally devastated Antony was grounded for his own safety, but used his time productively to develop a machine (the Fisher Trainer) to teach trainee pilots to shoot better. He was also an avid reader of *Reader's Digest*. Every copy was devoured, read aloud to his family, heavily underlined and kept in order in his study. His first child, Mark, recalls a wall of Antony's study lined with row upon row of years – decades even – of copies of *Reader's Digest*.

So how did our fighter pilot Fisher come across our academic Hayek? What follows is the story I have pieced together. Not all parts of it are accepted by all interested parties, but the pieces do fit. So this is my story and I'm sticking to it.

The marriage of true minds

The Road to Serfdom was published in March 1944 and, despite wartime paper shortages, it went through five reprints in the UK in 15 months. In spite of this, owing to wartime paper rationing, the publishers, Routledge, were unable to keep up with demand and Hayek complained that *The Road to Serfdom* had acquired a reputation for being 'that unobtainable book'.[4] It was such an incredible hit that Hayek lost track of the reviews and critics were moved to write whole books attacking him in both the UK and the US. Dr Laurence Hayek, only son of F. A. Hayek, owns his late father's own first edition copy of *The Road to Serfdom* as well as the printers' proof copy with Hayek's corrections. On the inside back cover of the former Hayek began listing the reviews as they came out. The list reads as follows:

Tablet	11/3/44	(Douglas Woodruff)
Sunday Times	12/3	(Harold Hobson one or two sentences)
	9/4	(G. M. Young)
Birmingham Post	14/3	(TWH)

---

4   Quoted in R. Cockett, *Thinking the Unthinkable: Think Tanks and the Economic Counter-Revolution, 1931–1983*, Fontana, London, 1995, p. 85.

Yorkshire Post	29/3	
Financial News	30/3	
Listener	30/3	
Daily Sketch	30/3	(Candidus)
Times Literary Supplement	1/4	
Spectator	31/3	(M. Polanyi)
Irish Times	25/3	
Observer	9/4	(George Orwell)
Manchester Guardian	19/4	(W)

But, as Hayek said to me in 1975, they started coming so fast he lost track and stopped recording them.

In early 1945 the University of Chicago Press published the US edition of *The Road to Serfdom* and, like Routledge in the UK, found themselves unable to meet the demand for copies owing to paper rationing. However, in April 1945 the book finally reached a mass audience when the *Reader's Digest* published their condensed version.[5] (Hayek thought it impossible to condense but always commented on what a great job the *Reader's Digest* editors did.) Whereas the book publishers had been dealing in issues of four or five thousand copies, the *Reader's Digest* had a print run which was measured in hundreds of thousands. For the first and still the only time, they put the condensed book at the front of the magazine where nobody could miss it – particularly a *Digest* junkie like Fisher.

The *Reader's Digest* appeared while Hayek was on board a ship en route to the USA for a lecture tour which had been arranged to

---

5   John Blundell discusses the contents of that issue of the *Reader's Digest* in detail in 'Looking back at the condensed version of *The Road to Serfdom* after 60 years', *Economic Affairs*, Vol. 24, No. 1.

coincide with the US book publication. He arrived to find himself a celebrity:

> ... I was told all our plans were changed: I would be going on a nationwide lecture tour beginning at NY Town Hall ... Imagine my surprise when they drove me there the next day and there were 3,000 people in the hall, plus a few score more in adjoining rooms with loudspeakers. There I was, with this battery of microphones and a veritable sea of expectant faces.[6]

Now I get to the detective work. That late spring/early summer of 1945 saw both Hayek and Fisher on the move. Hayek had spent the whole of the war at Cambridge but now it was safe for the LSE to return to London. Fisher had spent the war stationed all over the UK training pilots in gunnery and rising to the rank of Squadron Leader. He too was on the move to the War Office (now the Ministry of Defence) in central London, just a ten-minute walk from the LSE. Laurence Hayek and the LSE both confirm the dates of Hayek's move, while Fisher's RAF record, recently obtained from the Ministry of Defence by his elder son Mark, clearly dates his.

Forty years later both Hayek and Fisher were not overly helpful about exactly what happened next. Hayek in particular used to claim he had absolutely *no* recollection *whatsoever* of Fisher ever coming to him for advice. Fisher on the other hand was always very clear and very consistent about the dialogue – almost verbatim – but not so helpful on exactly how it happened. Here is how I believe it came about.

---

6   Interview with Hayek in *The Times*, 5 May 1985, quoted in Cockett, op. cit., pp. 100–101.

Fisher, the *Digest* junkie, is already politically active and is also worried about the future for his country. The April 1945 edition lands on his desk as he is moving to London and, after reading the cover story, he notes on the front that the author is at the University of London. A phone call establishes that the LSE is back in place and, one lunchtime or late one afternoon, Fisher makes the short walk from his office to the LSE and knocks on Hayek's door. Fisher also recalled the physical setting of Hayek's office in minute and accurate detail, including its proximity to that of the dreaded Harold Laski. Fisher claimed that after small talk (which neither excelled at) the conversation went like this:

Fisher I share all your worries and concerns as expressed in *The Road to Serfdom* and I'm going to go into politics and put it all right.

Hayek No you're not! Society's course will be changed only by a change in ideas. First you must reach the intellectuals, the teachers and writers, with reasoned argument. It will be *their* influence on society which will prevail, and the politicians will follow.

I have this quote framed above my desk alongside Keynes's famous line: 'The ideas of economists and political philosophers, both when they are right and when they are wrong, are more powerful than is commonly understood. Indeed the world is ruled by little else. Practical men, who believe themselves to be quite exempt from any intellectual influences, are usually the slaves of some defunct economist.'[7]

---

7   Keynes, *The General Theory of Employment, Interest and Money*, op. cit., p. 383.

Finally on this issue, let me quote Fisher's own words of 3 July 1985 when he spoke at a party at the IEA to celebrate its 30th birthday. (This would have been the 30th anniversary of the IEA's first book in June 1955 rather than incorporation in November 1955 or the actual opening in 1957.) At that party in July 1985 Fisher said:

> It was quite a day for me when Friedrich Hayek gave me some advice which must be *40 years ago almost to the day* and which completely changed my life. Friedrich got me started ... and two of the things he said way back are the things which have kept the IEA on course. One is to keep out of politics and the other is to make an intellectual case ... if you can stick to these rules you keep out of a lot of trouble and apparently do a lot of good.

As I said, 30 years later, on countless occasions, Hayek did not dispute the event or disown the advice, he simply said he could not remember. But it is of course very Hayekian advice and very much in keeping with his classic essay 'The Intellectuals and Socialism', which came out just a few years later and which has just been republished by the IEA.[8] This was hardly a blueprint for action – 'reach the intellectuals' – and indeed the next decade saw little direct fallout from that conversation, although three American intellectual entrepreneurs who had also sought out Hayek did get the ball rolling in the US.

The road to the IEA

Hayek taught at the LSE, got divorced in Arkansas, remarried, moved to Chicago and wrote *The Constitution of Liberty*.

---

8   F. A. Hayek, *The Intellectuals and Socialism*, Rediscovered Riches No. 4, IEA, London, 1998.

Fisher tried stockbroking, became a farmer, wrote a very prescient monograph, 'The Case for Freedom',[9] imported the idea of factory-farming of chickens, championed liberty in many different campaigns, visited the US looking for institute models he could copy, published *The Free Convertibility of Sterling* by George Winder,[10] incorporated the Institute of Economic Affairs, hired Ralph Harris and, as he always did, having hired the talent let it rip with a very hands-off approach to management. (When in 1987 he entrusted to me the future of the Atlas Economic Research Foundation, the body dedicated to building new IEAs around the world, he made it very clear that he was there if I wanted his help but that he really did expect me to crack on on my own.)

To begin with, in the late 1950s, it was not at all clear what the IEA would do. The exchange control book by Winder had been short, easily understood and on a fairly narrow but important topic. It had sold out its 2,000 print run very quickly because of Henry Hazlitt's review in *Newsweek*. Unfortunately the printer who had also sold the book for Antony went bankrupt, and the 2,000 names and addresses of the purchasers were lost. But Fisher had visited the Foundation for Economic Education in Irvington-on-Hudson, New York, had been exposed to its magazine, *The Freeman*, and still adored *Reader's Digest*. Harris had been a party political man turned academic turned editorial writer, while Arthur Seldon, the first editorial director, had been a research assistant to the famous LSE economist Arnold Plant before becoming chief economist of a brewers' association. Out of this mish-mash of experiences – academic, business, political, journalistic – came the

---

9   A. Fisher, *The Case for Freedom*, Runnymede Press, London, undated.
10 G. Winder, *The Free Convertibility of Sterling*, The Batchworth Press for the Institute of Economic Affairs, London, 1955.

distinctive IEA approach of short monographs containing the very best economics in good, jargon-free English, written by academics (mostly) or quasi-academics, in language accessible to the layman but still of use to the expert.

In the early days it was hard to find authors, hard to raise money and hard to get reviews and sales. At times everybody had to down pens to raise money or quickly pick up pens to co-author a paper. The first clear success of this venture – inspired by *The Road to Serfdom*, advised by Hayek, implemented by Fisher and run by Harris and Seldon – was the repeal of Resale Price Maintenance in 1964, a fantastic reform. It effectively outlawed the prevailing practice by which manufacturers priced goods – they literally stamped the price on the article – and discounting was illegal. There was no such thing as shopping around. This change alienated the small-business vote and put the Tories out for six years, but it transformed the UK economy and allowed a nation of shopkeepers to spread their wings. It was clearly heralded by a 1960 IEA study, *Resale Price Maintenance and Shoppers' Choice* by Basil Yamey.[11] Other successes followed and the IEA's impetus grew, but what was happening to Hayek and Fisher?

Hayek had moved from Chicago back to Europe, and in December 1974 received the Nobel Prize. He was 75 and his health had not been good. He was also depressed. However the prize (and the big cheque) cheered him up no end.

Fisher had sold the chicken business for millions and had put a large part of his minority share into an experimental turtle farm in the Cayman Islands. Well, the experiment worked brilliantly but

---

11   B. S. Yamey, *Resale Price Maintenance and Shoppers' Choice,* Hobart Paper No. 1, IEA, London, 1960.

the environmentalists closed down his largest market – the US.[12] He refused to hide behind limited liability and used the balance of his fortune to pay off all debts.

1974 – now 30 years after *The Road to Serfdom* – was a big year for Fisher too, because, free from business concerns, he was able to respond to businessmen and others around the world who noted the IEA's growing influence and came to him for advice.

Sowing the seed

So the entrepreneur turned fighter pilot turned gunnery trainer turned stockbroker turned dairy farmer turned chicken pioneer turned turtle saviour became the Johnny Appleseed of the free-market movement, going all over the world and setting up new IEA-type operations.

First he joined the very young Fraser Institute in Vancouver, BC; quickly moved on to help Greg Lindsay and the Centre for Independent Studies in Australia; hired David Theroux, recently departed from the Cato Institute, to set up the Pacific Research Institute in San Francisco; gave support to the Butler brothers and Madsen Pirie as they founded the Adam Smith Institute in London; and incorporated with William Casey the Manhattan Institute where, as they did so, they sat on movers' boxes in an otherwise empty office.

It took ten years to give birth to Institute No. 1 – the IEA. For all but twenty years it was the only one in the family; in just six years five more were born, and then the fun really started. In 1981

---

12 For a full account see P. and S. Fosdick, *Last Chance Lost: Can and Should Farming Save the Green Sea Turtle?*, Irvin S. Naylor, York, PA, 1994.

Fisher incorporated the Atlas Economic Research Foundation to be a focal point for institutes and to channel funds to start-ups. By the time of his death in 1988 we listed 30-plus institutes in 20 or so countries. By 1991 we were listing 80 and I now count about 100 in 76 countries.

All of this can be traced back to this young economist, his book, the *Reader's Digest* condensation, and a young RAF officer … through the IEA … through CIS/PRI/ASI/Manhattan and Fraser … to 100 institutes in 76 countries today, who together are literally changing the world.

To illustrate our impact, let me finish with a story from Lord Howell of Guildford, a minister in the 1980s. He came into my office recently and pointed at the big boardroom table where I work every day and which was donated by Antony in the late 1960s. Howell said: 'You know, John, it was at that table that we first got serious about privatisation in 1968. The idea fizzled in the 1970s, took off in the 1980s and in the 1990s burns brightly around the world.' I replied: 'Yes, it burns so brightly that last year world-wide privatisation revenues topped $100 billion for the first time.'

So it is quite a story we have to tell and it all begins here with the condensed version of *The Road to Serfdom* and the cartoon version drawn to my attention only recently by Laurence Hayek. Read the condensed version, now published in our 'Rediscovered Riches' series for the first time since its original appearance in the *Reader's Digest*, and wonder on all the changes it led to: all the misery avoided and all the prosperity created.

JOHN BLUNDELL

November 1999

PREFACE TO THE *READER'S DIGEST* CONDENSED VERSION OF *THE ROAD TO SERFDOM*

'In *The Road to Serfdom*', writes Henry Hazlitt in the *New York Times*, 'Friedrich A. Hayek has written one of the most important books of our generation. It restates for our time the issue between liberty and authority. It is an arresting call to all well-intentioned planners and socialists, to all those who are sincere democrats and liberals at heart, to stop, look and listen.'

The author is an internationally known economist. An Austrian by birth, he was director of the Austrian Institute for Economic Research and lecturer in economics at the University of Vienna during the years of the rise of fascism in Central Europe. He has lived in England since 1931 when he became Professor of Economic Science at the University of London, and is now a British citizen.

Professor Hayek, with great power and rigour of reasoning, sounds a grim warning to Americans and Britons who look to the government to provide the way out of all our economic difficulties. He demonstrates that fascism and what the Germans correctly call National Socialism are the inevitable results of the increasing growth of state control and state power, of national 'planning' and of socialism.

In a foreword to *The Road to Serfdom* John Chamberlain, book editor of *Harper's*, writes: 'This book is a warning cry in a time of hesitation. It says to us: Stop, look and listen. Its logic is incontestable, and it should have the widest possible audience.'

SUMMARY

(Jacket notes written by Hayek for the first edition)

- Is there a greater tragedy imaginable than that in our endeavour consciously to shape our future in accordance with high ideals we should in fact unwittingly produce the very opposite of what we have been striving for?
- The contention that only the peculiar wickedness of the Germans has produced the Nazi system is likely to become the excuse for forcing on us the very institutions which have produced that wickedness.
- Totalitarianism is the new word we have adopted to describe the unexpected but nevertheless inseparable manifestations of what in theory we call socialism.
- In a planned system we cannot confine collective action to the tasks on which we agree, but are forced to produce agreement on everything in order that any action can be taken at all.
- The more the state 'plans' the more difficult planning becomes for the individual.
- The economic freedom which is the prerequisite of any other freedom cannot be the freedom from economic care which the socialists promise us and which can be obtained only by relieving the individual at the same time of the necessity and of the power of choice: it must be the freedom of economic activity which, with the right of choice, inevitably also carries the risk and the responsibility of that right.

- What our generation has forgotten is that the system of private property is the most important guarantee of freedom, not only for those who own property, but scarcely less for those who do not.
- We shall never prevent the abuse of power if we are not prepared to limit power in a way which occasionally may prevent its use for desirable purposes.
- We shall all be the gainers if we can create a world fit for small states to live in.
- The first need is to free ourselves of that worst form of contemporary obscurantism which tries to persuade us that what we have done in the recent past was all either wise or unavoidable. We shall not grow wiser before we learn that much that we have done was very foolish.

The *Reader's Digest* condensed version of
The Road to Serfdom

THE ROAD TO SERFDOM

(condensed version, published in the *Reader's Digest*,
April 1945 edition)

The author has spent about half his adult life in his native
Austria, in close touch with German thought, and the other half in
the United States and England. In the latter period he has become
increasingly convinced that some of the forces which destroyed
freedom in Germany are also at work here.

The very magnitude of the outrages committed by the National
Socialists has strengthened the assurance that a totalitarian
system cannot happen here. But let us remember that 15 years ago
the possibility of such a thing happening in Germany would have
appeared just as fantastic not only to nine-tenths of the Germans
themselves, but also to the most hostile foreign observer.

There are many features which were then regarded as 'typically
German' which are now equally familiar in America and England,
and many symptoms that point to a further development in the
same direction: the increasing veneration for the state, the fatal-
istic acceptance of 'inevitable trends', the enthusiasm for 'organization' of everything (we now call it 'planning').

The character of the danger is, if possible, even less understood
here than it was in Germany. The supreme tragedy is still not seen
that in Germany it was largely people of good will who, by their
socialist policies, prepared the way for the forces which stand
for everything they detest. Few recognize that the rise of fascism
and Marxism was not a reaction against the socialist trends of the

preceding period *but a necessary outcome of those tendencies*. Yet it is significant that many of the leaders of these movements, from Mussolini down (and including Laval and Quisling) began as socialists and ended as fascists or Nazis.

In the democracies at present, many who sincerely hate all of Nazism's manifestations are working for ideals whose realization would lead straight to the abhorred tyranny. Most of the people whose views influence developments are in some measure socialists. They believe that our economic life should be 'consciously directed', that we should substitute 'economic planning' for the competitive system. Yet is there a greater tragedy imaginable than that, in our endeavour consciously to shape our future in accordance with high ideals, we should in fact unwittingly produce the very opposite of what we have been striving for?

Planning and power

In order to achieve their ends the planners must create power – power over men wielded by other men – of a magnitude never before known. Their success will depend on the extent to which they achieve such power. Democracy is an obstacle to this suppression of freedom which the centralized direction of economic activity requires. Hence arises the clash between planning and democracy.

Many socialists have the tragic illusion that by depriving private individuals of the power they possess in an individualist system, and transferring this power to society, they thereby extinguish power. What they overlook is that by concentrating power so that it can be used in the service of a single plan, it is not merely transformed, but infinitely heightened. By uniting in the hands of some single body power formerly exercised independently by many, an amount of power is created infinitely greater than any that existed before, so much more far-reaching as almost to be different in kind.

It is entirely fallacious to argue that the great power exercised by a central planning board would be 'no greater than the power collectively exercised by private boards of directors'. There is, in a competitive society, nobody who can exercise even a fraction of the power which a socialist planning board would possess. To decentralize power is to reduce the absolute amount of power, and the competitive system is the only system designed to minimize the power exercised by man over man. Who can seriously doubt that the power which a millionaire, who may be my employer, has over me is very much less than that which the smallest bureaucrat possesses who wields the coercive power of the state and on whose discretion it depends how I am allowed to live and work?

In every real sense a badly paid unskilled workman in this country has more freedom to shape his life than many an employer in Germany or a much better paid engineer or manager in Russia. If he wants to change his job or the place where he lives, if he wants to profess certain views or spend his leisure in a particular way, he faces no absolute impediments. There are no dangers to bodily security and freedom that confine him by brute force to the task and environment to which a superior has assigned him.

Our generation has forgotten that the system of private property is the most important guarantee of freedom. It is only because the control of the means of production is divided among many people acting independently that we as individuals can decide what to do with ourselves. When all the means of production are vested in a single hand, whether it be nominally that of 'society' as a whole or that of a dictator, whoever exercises this control has complete power over us. In the hands of private individuals, what is called economic power can be an instrument of coercion, but it is never control over the whole life of a person. But when economic power is centralized as an instrument of political power it creates a degree of dependence scarcely distinguishable from slavery. It has been well said that, in a country where the sole employer is the state, opposition means death by slow starvation.

Background to danger

Individualism, in contrast to socialism and all other forms of totalitarianism, is based on the respect of Christianity for the individual man and the belief that it is desirable that men should be free to develop their own individual gifts and bents. This philosophy, first fully developed during the Renaissance, grew and spread into what we know as Western civilization. The general direction of social development was one of freeing the individual from the ties which bound him in feudal society.

Perhaps the greatest result of this unchaining of individual energies was the marvellous growth of science. Only since industrial freedom opened the path to the free use of new knowledge, only since everything could be tried – if somebody could be found to back it at his own risk – has science made the great strides which in the last 150 years have changed the face of the world. The result of this growth surpassed all expectations. Wherever the barriers to the free exercise of human ingenuity were removed, man became rapidly able to satisfy ever-widening ranges of desire. By the beginning of the twentieth century the working man in the Western world had reached a degree of material comfort, security and personal independence which 100 years before had hardly seemed possible.

The effect of this success was to create among men a new sense of power over their own fate, the belief in the unbounded possibilities of improving their own lot. What had been achieved came to be regarded as a secure and imperishable possession, acquired once and for all; and the rate of progress began to seem too slow. Moreover the principles which had made this progress possible came to be regarded as obstacles to speedier progress, impatiently to be brushed away. It might be said that the very success of liberalism became the cause of its decline.

No sensible person should have doubted that the economic principles of the nineteenth century were only a beginning – that there were immense possibilities of advancement on the lines on which we had moved. But according to the views now dominant, the question is no longer how we can make the best use of the spontaneous forces found in a free society. We have in effect undertaken to dispense with these forces and to replace them by collective and 'conscious' direction.

It is significant that this abandonment of liberalism, whether expressed as socialism in its more radical form or merely as 'organization' or 'planning', was perfected in Germany. During the last quarter of the nineteenth century and the first quarter of the twentieth, Germany moved far ahead in both the theory and the practice of socialism, so that even today Russian discussion largely carries on where the Germans left off. The Germans, long before the Nazis, were attacking liberalism and democracy, capitalism, and individualism.

Long before the Nazis, too, the German and Italian socialists were using techniques of which the Nazis and fascists later made effective use. The idea of a political party which embraces all activities of the individual from the cradle to the grave, which claims to guide his views on everything, was first put into practice by the socialists. It was not the fascists but the socialists who began to collect children at the tenderest age into political organizations to direct their thinking. It was not the fascists but the socialists who first thought of organizing sports and games, football and hiking, in party clubs where the members would not be infected by other views. It was the socialists who first insisted that the party member should distinguish himself from others by the modes of greeting and the forms of address. It was they who, by their organization of 'cells' and devices for the permanent supervision of private life, created the prototype of the totalitarian party.

By the time Hitler came to power, liberalism was dead in Germany. And it was socialism that had killed it.

To many who have watched the transition from socialism to fascism at close quarters the connection between the two systems has become increasingly obvious, but in the democracies the majority of people still believe that socialism and freedom can be combined. They do not realize that democratic socialism, the great utopia of the last few generations, is not only unachievable, but that to strive for it produces something utterly different – the very destruction of freedom itself. As has been aptly said: 'What has always made the state a hell on earth has been precisely that man has tried to make it his heaven.'

It is disquieting to see in England and the United States today the same drawing together of forces and nearly the same contempt of all that is liberal in the old sense. 'Conservative socialism' was the slogan under which a large number of writers prepared the atmosphere in which National Socialism succeeded. It is 'conservative socialism' which is the dominant trend among us now.

The liberal way of planning

'Planning' owes its popularity largely to the fact that everybody desires, of course, that we should handle our common problems with as much foresight as possible. The dispute between the modern planners and the liberals is *not* on whether we ought to employ systematic thinking in planning our affairs. It is a dispute about what is the best way of so doing. The question is whether we should create conditions under which the knowledge and initiative of individuals are given the best scope so that *they* can plan most successfully; or whether we should direct and organize all economic activities according to a 'blueprint', that is, 'consciously direct the resources of society to conform to the planners' particular views of who should have what'.

It is important not to confuse opposition against the latter kind of planning with a dogmatic *laissez faire* attitude. The liberal argument does not advocate leaving things just as they are; it favours making the best possible use of the forces of competition as a means of coordinating human efforts. It is based on the conviction that, where effective competition can be created, it is a better way of guiding individual efforts than any other. It emphasizes that in order to make competition work beneficially a carefully thought-out legal framework is required, and that neither the past nor the existing legal rules are free from grave defects.

Liberalism is opposed, however, to supplanting competition by inferior methods of guiding economic activity. And it regards competition as superior not only because in most circumstances it is the most efficient method known but because *it is the only method which does not require the coercive or arbitrary intervention of authority*. It dispenses with the need for 'conscious social control' and gives individuals a chance to decide whether the prospects of a particular occupation are sufficient to compensate for the disadvantages connected with it.

The successful use of competition does not preclude some types of government interference. For instance, to limit working hours, to require certain sanitary arrangements, to provide an extensive system of social services is fully compatible with the preservation of competition. There are, too, certain fields where the system of competition is impracticable. For example, the harmful effects of deforestation or of the smoke of factories cannot be confined to the owner of the property in question. But the fact that we have to resort to direct regulation by authority where the conditions for the proper working of competition cannot be created does not prove that we should suppress competition where it can be made to function. To create conditions in which competition will be as effective as possible, to prevent fraud and deception, to break up monopolies – these tasks provide a wide and unquestioned field for state activity.

This does not mean that it is possible to find some 'middle way' between competition and central direction, though nothing seems at first more plausible, or is more likely to appeal to reasonable people. Mere common sense proves a treacherous guide in this field. Although competition can bear some mixture of regulation, it cannot be combined with planning to any extent we like without ceasing to operate as an effective guide to production. Both competition and central direction become poor and inefficient tools if they are incomplete, and a mixture of the two means that neither will work.

Planning and competition can be combined only by planning *for* competition, not by planning *against* competition. The planning against which all our criticism is directed is solely the planning against competition.

The great utopia

There can be no doubt that most of those in the democracies who demand a central direction of all economic activity still believe that socialism and individual freedom can be combined. Yet socialism was early recognized by many thinkers as the gravest threat to freedom.

It is rarely remembered now that socialism in its beginnings was frankly authoritarian. It began quite openly as a reaction against the liberalism of the French Revolution. The French writers who laid its foundation had no doubt that their ideas could be put into practice only by a strong dictatorial government. The first of modern planners, Saint-Simon, predicted that those who did not obey his proposed planning boards would be 'treated as cattle'.

Nobody saw more clearly than the great political thinker de Tocqueville that democracy stands in an irreconcilable conflict with socialism: 'Democracy extends the sphere of individual freedom,' he said. 'Democracy attaches all possible value to each man,' he said in 1848, 'while socialism makes each man a mere agent, a mere number. Democracy and socialism have nothing in common but one word: equality. But notice the difference: while democracy seeks equality in liberty, socialism seeks equality in restraint and servitude.'

To allay these suspicions and to harness to its cart the strongest of all political motives – the craving for freedom – socialists began increasingly to make use of the promise of a 'new freedom'. Socialism was to bring 'economic freedom' without which political freedom was 'not worth having'.

To make this argument sound plausible, the word 'freedom' was subjected to a subtle change in meaning. The word had formerly meant freedom from coercion, from the arbitrary power of other men. Now it was made to mean freedom from necessity, release from the compulsion of the circumstances which inevitably limit the range of choice of all of us. Freedom in this sense is, of course, merely another name for power or wealth. The demand for the new freedom was thus only another name for the old demand for a redistribution of wealth.

The claim that a planned economy would produce a substantially larger output than the competitive system is being progressively abandoned by most students of the problem. Yet it is this false hope as much as anything which drives us along the road to planning.

Although our modern socialists' promise of greater freedom is genuine and sincere, in recent years observer after observer has been impressed by the unforeseen consequences of socialism, the extraordinary similarity in many respects of the conditions under 'communism' and 'fascism'. As the writer Peter Drucker expressed it in 1939, 'the complete collapse of the belief in the attainability of freedom and equality through Marxism has forced Russia to travel the same road toward a totalitarian society of unfreedom and inequality which Germany has been following. Not that communism and fascism are essentially the same. Fascism is the stage reached after communism has proved an illusion, and it has proved as much an illusion in Russia as in pre-Hitler Germany.'

No less significant is the intellectual outlook of the rank and file in the communist and fascist movements in Germany before 1933. The relative ease with which a young communist could be converted into a Nazi or vice versa was well known, best of all to the propagandists of the two parties. The communists and Nazis clashed more frequently with each other than with other parties simply because they competed for the same type of mind and reserved for each other the hatred of the heretic. Their practice showed how closely they are related. To both, the real enemy, the man with whom they had nothing in common, was the liberal of the old type. While to the Nazi the communist and to the communist the Nazi, and to both the socialist, are potential recruits made of the right timber, they both know that there can be no compromise between them and those who really believe in individual freedom.

What is promised to us as the Road to Freedom is in fact the Highroad to Servitude. For it is not difficult to see what must be the consequences when democracy embarks upon a course of planning. The goal of the planning will be described by some such vague term as 'the general welfare'. There will be no real agreement as to the ends to be attained, and the effect of the people's agreeing that there must be central planning, without agreeing on the ends, will be rather as if a group of people were to commit themselves to take a journey together without agreeing where they want to go: with the result that they may all have to make a journey which most of them do not want at all.

Democratic assemblies cannot function as planning agencies. They cannot produce agreement on everything – the whole direction of the resources of the nation – for the number of possible courses of action will be legion. Even if a congress could, by proceeding step by step and compromising at each point, agree on some scheme, it would certainly in the end satisfy nobody.

To draw up an economic plan in this fashion is even less possible than, for instance, successfully to plan a military campaign by democratic procedure. As in strategy, it would become inevitable to delegate the task to experts. And even if, by this expedient, a democracy should succeed in planning every sector of economic activity, it would still have to face the problem of integrating these separate plans into a unitary whole. There will be a stronger and stronger demand that some board or some single individual should be given powers to act on their own responsibility. The cry for an economic dictator is a characteristic stage in the movement toward planning.

Thus the legislative body will be reduced to choosing the persons who are to have practically absolute power. The whole system will tend toward that kind of dictatorship in which the head of government is from time to time confirmed in his position by popular vote, but where he has all the power at his command to make certain that the vote will go in the direction that he desires.

Planning leads to dictatorship because dictatorship is the most effective instrument of coercion and, as such, essential if central planning on a large scale is to be possible. There is no justification for the widespread belief that, so long as power is conferred by democratic procedure, it cannot be arbitrary; it is not the source of power which prevents it from being arbitrary; to be free from dictatorial qualities, the power must also be limited. A true 'dictatorship of the proletariat', even if democratic in form, if it undertook centrally to direct the economic system, would probably destroy personal freedom as completely as any autocracy has ever done.

Individual freedom cannot be reconciled with the supremacy of one single purpose to which the whole of society is permanently subordinated. To a limited extent we ourselves experience this fact in wartime, when subordination of almost everything to the immediate and pressing need is the price at which we preserve our freedom in the long run. The fashionable phrases about doing for the purposes of peace what we have learned to do for the purposes of war are completely misleading, for it is sensible temporarily to sacrifice freedom in order to make it more secure in the future, but it is quite a different thing to sacrifice liberty permanently in the interests of a planned economy.

To those who have watched the transition from socialism to fascism at close quarters, the connection between the two systems is obvious. The realization of the socialist programme means the destruction of freedom. Democratic socialism, the great utopia of the last few generations, is simply not achievable.

Why the worst get on top

No doubt an American or English 'fascist' system would greatly differ from the Italian or German models; no doubt, if the transition were effected without violence, we might expect to get a better type of leader. Yet this does not mean that our fascist system would in the end prove very different or much less intolerable than its prototypes. There are strong reasons for believing that the worst features of the totalitarian systems are phenomena which totalitarianism is certain sooner or later to produce.

Just as the democratic statesman who sets out to plan economic life will soon be confronted with the alternative of either assuming dictatorial powers or abandoning his plans, so the totalitarian leader would soon have to choose between disregard of ordinary morals and failure. It is for this reason that the unscrupulous are likely to be more successful in a society tending toward totalitarianism. Who does not see this has not yet grasped the full width of the gulf which separates totalitarianism from the essentially individualist Western civilization.

The totalitarian leader must collect around him a group which is prepared voluntarily to submit to that discipline they are to impose by force upon the rest of the people. That socialism can be put into practice only by methods of which most socialists disapprove is, of course, a lesson learned by many social reformers in the past. The old socialist parties were inhibited by their democratic ideals; they did not possess the ruthlessness required for the performance of their chosen task. It is characteristic that both in Germany and in Italy the success of fascism was preceded by the refusal of the socialist parties to take over the respons-ibilities of government. They were unwilling wholeheartedly to employ the methods to which they had pointed the way. They still hoped for the miracle of a majority's agreeing on a particular plan for the organization of the whole of society. Others had already learned the lesson that in a planned society the question can no longer be on what do a majority of the people agree but what the largest single group is whose members agree sufficiently to make unified direction of all affairs possible.

There are three main reasons why such a numerous group, with fairly similar views, is not likely to be formed by the best but rather by the worst elements of any society.

First, the higher the education and intelligence of individuals become, the more their tastes and views are differentiated. If we wish to find a high degree of uniformity in outlook, we have to descend to the regions of lower moral and intellectual standards where the more primitive instincts prevail. This does not mean that the majority of people have low moral standards; it merely means that the largest group of people whose values are very similar are the people with low standards.

Second, since this group is not large enough to give sufficient weight to the leader's endeavours, he will have to increase their numbers by converting more to the same simple creed. He must gain the support of the docile and gullible, who have no strong convictions of their own but are ready to accept a ready-made system of values if it is only drummed into their ears sufficiently loudly and frequently. It will be those whose vague and imperfectly formed ideas are easily swayed and whose passions and emotions are readily aroused who will thus swell the ranks of the totalitarian party.

Third, to weld together a closely coherent body of supporters, the leader must appeal to a common human weakness. It seems to be easier for people to agree on a negative programme – on the hatred of an enemy, on the envy of the better off – than on any positive task.

The contrast between the 'we' and the 'they' is consequently always employed by those who seek the allegiance of huge masses. The enemy may be internal, like the 'Jew' in Germany or the 'kulak' in Russia, or he may be external. In any case, this technique has the great advantage of leaving the leader greater freedom of action than would almost any positive programme.

Advancement within a totalitarian group or party depends largely on a willingness to do immoral things. The principle that the end justifies the means, which in individualist ethics is regarded as the denial of all morals, in collectivist ethics becomes necessarily the supreme rule. There is literally nothing which the consistent collectivist must not be prepared to do if it serves 'the good of the whole', because that is to him the only criterion of what ought to be done.

Once you admit that the individual is merely a means to serve the ends of the higher entity called society or the nation, most of those features of totalitarianism which horrify us follow of necessity. From the collectivist standpoint intolerance and brutal suppression of dissent, deception and spying, the complete disregard of the life and happiness of the individual are essential and unavoidable. Acts which revolt all our feelings, such as the shooting of hostages or the killing of the old or sick, are treated as mere matters of expediency; the compulsory uprooting and transportation of hundreds of thousands becomes an instrument of policy approved by almost everybody except the victims.

To be a useful assistant in the running of a totalitarian state, therefore, a man must be prepared to break every moral rule he has ever known if this seems necessary to achieve the end set for him. In the totalitarian machine there will be special opportunities for the ruthless and unscrupulous. Neither the Gestapo nor the administration of a concentration camp, neither the Ministry of Propaganda nor the SA or SS (or their Russian counterparts) are suitable places for the exercise of humanitarian feelings. Yet it is through such positions that the road to the highest positions in the totalitarian state leads.

A distinguished American economist, Professor Frank H. Knight, correctly notes that the authorities of a collectivist state 'would have to do these things whether they wanted to or not: and the probability of the people in power being individuals who would dislike the possession and exercise of power is on a level with the probability that an extremely tender-hearted person would get the job of whipping master in a slave plantation'.

A further point should be made here: collectivism means the end of truth. To make a totalitarian system function efficiently it is not enough that everybody should be forced to work for the ends selected by those in control; it is essential that the people should come to regard these ends as their own. This is brought about by propaganda and by complete control of all sources of information.

The most effective way of making people accept the validity of the values they are to serve is to persuade them that they are really the same as those they have always held, but which were not properly understood or recognized before. And the most efficient technique to this end is to use the old words but change their meaning. Few traits of totalitarian regimes are at the same time so confusing to the superficial observer and yet so characteristic of the whole intellectual climate as this complete perversion of language.

The worst sufferer in this respect is the word 'liberty'. It is a word used as freely in totalitarian states as elsewhere. Indeed, it could almost be said that wherever liberty as we know it has been destroyed, this has been done in the name of some new freedom promised to the people. Even among us we have planners who promise us a 'collective freedom', which is as misleading as anything said by totalitarian politicians. 'Collective freedom' is not the freedom of the members of society, but the unlimited freedom of the planner to do with society that which he pleases. This is the confusion of freedom with power carried to the extreme.

It is not difficult to deprive the great majority of independent thought. But the minority who will retain an inclination to criticize must also be silenced. Public criticism or even expressions of doubt must be suppressed because they tend to weaken support of the regime. As Sidney and Beatrice Webb report of the position in every Russian enterprise: 'Whilst the work is in progress, any public expression of doubt that the plan will be successful is an act of disloyalty and even of treachery because of its possible effect on the will and efforts of the rest of the staff.'

Control extends even to subjects which seem to have no political significance. The theory of relativity, for instance, has been opposed as a 'Semitic attack on the foundation of Christian and Nordic physics' and because it is 'in conflict with dialectical materialism and Marxist dogma'. *Every* activity must derive its justification from conscious social purpose. There must be no spontaneous, unguided activity, because it might produce results which cannot be foreseen and for which the plan does not provide.

The principle extends even to games and amusements. I leave it to the reader to guess where it was that chess players were officially exhorted that 'we must finish once and for all with the neutrality of chess. We must condemn once and for all the formula chess for the sake of chess.'

Perhaps the most alarming fact is that contempt for intellectual liberty is not a thing which arises only once the totalitarian system is established, but can be found everywhere among those who have embraced a collectivist faith. The worst oppression is condoned if it is committed in the name of socialism. Intolerance of opposing ideas is openly extolled. The tragedy of collectivist thought is that while it starts out to make reason supreme, it ends by destroying reason.

There is one aspect of the change in moral values brought about by the advance of collectivism which provides special food for thought. It is that the virtues which are held less and less in esteem in Britain and America are precisely those on which Anglo-Saxons justly prided themselves and in which they were generally recognized to excel. These virtues were independence and self-reliance, individual initiative and local responsibility, the successful reliance on voluntary activity, non-interference with one's neighbour and tolerance of the different, and a healthy suspicion of power and authority.

Almost all the traditions and institutions which have moulded the national character and the whole moral climate of England

and America are those which the progress of collectivism and its centralistic tendencies are progressively destroying.

Planning vs. the Rule of Law

Nothing distinguishes more clearly a free country from a country under arbitrary government than the observance in the former of the great principles known as the Rule of Law. Stripped of technicalities this means that government in all its actions is bound by rules fixed and announced beforehand – rules that make it possible to foresee with fair certainty how the authority will use its coercive powers in given circumstances and to plan one's individual affairs on the basis of this knowledge. Thus, within the known rules of the game, the individual is free to pursue his personal ends, certain that the powers of government will not be used deliberately to frustrate his efforts.

Socialist economic planning necessarily involves the very opposite of this. The planning authority cannot tie itself down in advance to general rules which prevent arbitrariness.

When the government has to decide how many pigs are to be raised or how many buses are to run, which coal-mines are to operate, or at what prices shoes are to be sold, these decisions cannot be settled for long periods in advance. They depend inevitably on the circumstances of the moment, and in making such decisions it will always be necessary to balance, one against the other, the interests of various persons and groups.

In the end somebody's views will have to decide whose interests are more important, and these views must become part of the law of the land. Hence the familiar fact that the more the state 'plans', the more difficult planning becomes for the individual.

The difference between the two kinds of rule is important. It is the same as that between providing signposts and commanding people which road to take.

Moreover, under central planning the government cannot be impartial. The state ceases to be a piece of utilitarian machinery intended to help individuals in the fullest development of their individual personality and becomes an institution which deliberately discriminates between particular needs of different people, and allows one man to do what another must be prevented from doing. It must lay down by a legal rule how well off particular people shall be and what different people are to be allowed to have.

The Rule of Law, the absence of legal privileges of particular people designated by authority, is what safeguards that equality before the law which is the opposite of arbitrary government. It is significant that socialists (and Nazis) have always protested against 'merely' formal justice, that they have objected to law which had no views on how well off particular people ought to be, that they have demanded a 'socialization of the law' and attacked the independence of judges.

In a planned society the law must legalize what to all intents and purposes remains arbitrary action. If the law says that such a board or authority may do what it pleases, anything that board or authority does is legal – but its actions are certainly not subject to the Rule of Law. By giving the government unlimited powers the most arbitrary rule can be made legal; and in this way a democracy may set up the most complete despotism imaginable.

The Rule of Law was consciously evolved only during the liberal age and is one of its greatest achievements. It is the legal embodiment of freedom. As Immanuel Kant put it, 'Man is free if he needs obey no person but solely the laws.'

Is planning 'inevitable'?

It is revealing that few planners today are content to say that central planning is desirable. Most of them affirm that we now are compelled to it by circumstances beyond our control.

One argument frequently heard is that the complexity of modern civilization creates new problems with which we cannot hope to deal effectively except by central planning. This argument is based upon a complete misapprehension of the working of competition. The very complexity of modern conditions makes competition the only method by which a coordination of affairs can be adequately achieved.

There would be no difficulty about efficient control or planning were conditions so simple that a single person or board could effectively survey all the facts. But as the factors which have to be taken into account become numerous and complex, no one centre can keep track of them. The constantly changing conditions of demand and supply of different commodities can never be fully known or quickly enough disseminated by any one centre.

Under competition – and under no other economic order – the price system automatically records all the relevant data. Entrepreneurs, by watching the movement of comparatively few prices, as an engineer watches a few dials, can adjust their activities to those of their fellows.

Compared with this method of solving the economic problem – by decentralization plus automatic coordination through the price system – the method of central direction is incredibly clumsy, primitive, and limited in scope. It is no exaggeration to say that if we had had to rely on central planning for the growth of our industrial system, it would never have reached the degree of differentiation and flexibility it has attained. Modern civilization has been possible precisely because it did not have to be consciously created. The division of labour has gone far beyond what could have been planned. Any further growth in economic complexity, far from making central direction more necessary, makes it more important than ever that we should use the technique of competition and not depend on conscious control.

It is also argued that technological changes have made competition impossible in a constantly increasing number of fields and that our only choice is between control of production by private monopolies and direction by the government. The growth of monopoly, however, seems not so much a necessary consequence of the advance of technology as the result of the policies pursued in most countries.

The most comprehensive study of this situation is that by the Temporary National Economic Committee, which certainly cannot be accused of an unduly liberal bias. The committee concludes:

> The superior efficiency of large establishments has not been demonstrated; the advantages that are supposed to destroy competition have failed to manifest themselves in many fields ... the conclusion that the advantage of large-scale production must lead inevitably to the abolition of competition cannot be accepted ... It should be noted, moreover, that monopoly is frequently attained through collusive agreement and promoted by public policies. When these agreements are invalidated and these policies reversed, competitive conditions can be restored.

Anyone who has observed how aspiring monopolists regularly seek the assistance of the state to make their control effective can have little doubt that there is nothing inevitable about this development. In the United States a highly protectionist policy aided the growth of monopolies. In Germany the growth of cartels has since 1878 been systematically fostered by deliberate policy. It was here that, with the help of the state, the first great experiment in 'scientific planning' and 'conscious organization of industry' led to the creation of giant monopolies. The suppression of competition was a matter of deliberate policy in Germany, undertaken in the service of an ideal which we now call planning.

Great danger lies in the policies of two powerful groups, organized capital and organized labour, which support the monopolistic organization of industry. The recent growth of monopoly is largely the result of a deliberate collaboration of organized capital and organized labour where the privileged groups of labour share in the monopoly profits at the expense of the community and particularly at the expense of those employed in the less well organized industries. However, there is no reason to believe that this movement is inevitable.

The movement toward planning is the result of deliberate action. No external necessities force us to it.

Can planning free us from care?

Most planners who have seriously considered the practical aspects of their task have little doubt that a directed economy must be run on dictatorial lines, that the complex system of interrelated activities must be directed by staffs of experts, with ultimate power in the hands of a commander-in-chief whose actions must not be fettered by democratic procedure. The consolation our planners offer us is that this authoritarian direction will apply 'only' to economic matters. This assurance is usually accompanied by the suggestion that, by giving up freedom in the less important aspects of our lives, we shall obtain freedom in the pursuit of higher values. On this ground people who abhor the idea of a political dictatorship often clamour for a dictator in the economic field.

The arguments used appeal to our best instincts. If planning really did free us from less important cares and so made it easier to render our existence one of plain living and high thinking, who would wish to belittle such an ideal?

Unfortunately, purely economic ends cannot be separated from the other ends of life. What is misleadingly called the 'economic motive' means merely the desire for general opportunity. If we strive for money, it is because money offers us the widest choice in enjoying the fruits of our efforts – once earned, we are free to spend the money as we wish.

Because it is through the limitation of our money incomes that we feel the restrictions which our relative poverty still imposes on us, many have come to hate money as the symbol of these restrictions. Actually, money is one of the greatest instruments of freedom ever invented by man. It is money which in existing society opens an astounding range of choice to the poor man – a range greater than that which not many generations ago was open to the wealthy.

We shall better understand the significance of the service of money if we consider what it would really mean if, as so many socialists characteristically propose, the 'pecuniary motive' were largely displaced by 'non-economic incentives'. If all rewards, instead of being offered in money, were offered in the form of public distinctions, or privileges, positions of power over other men, better housing or food, opportunities for travel or education, this would merely mean that the recipient would no longer be allowed to choose, and that whoever fixed the reward would determine not only its size but the way in which it should be enjoyed.

The so-called economic freedom which the planners promise us means precisely that we are to be relieved of the necessity of solving our own economic problems and that the bitter choices which this often involves are to be made for us. Since under modern conditions we are for almost everything dependent on means which our fellow men provide, economic planning would involve direction of almost the whole of our life. There is hardly an aspect of it, from our primary needs to our relations with our family and friends, from the nature of our work to the use of our leisure, over which the planner would not exercise his 'conscious control'.

The power of the planner over our private lives would be hardly less effective if the consumer were nominally free to spend his income as he pleased, for the authority would control production.

Our freedom of choice in a competitive society rests on the fact that, if one person refuses to satisfy our wishes, we can turn to another. But if we face a monopolist we are at his mercy. And an authority directing the whole economic system would be the most powerful monopolist imaginable.

It would have complete power to decide what we are to be given and on what terms. It would not only decide what commodities and services are to be available and in what quantities; it would be able to direct their distribution between districts and groups and could, if it wished, discriminate between persons to any degree it liked. Not our own view, but somebody else's view of what we ought to like or dislike, would determine what we should get.

The will of the authority would shape and 'guide' our daily lives even more in our position as producers. For most of us the time we spend at our work is a large part of our whole lives, and our job usually determines the place where and the people among whom we live. Hence some freedom in choosing our work is probably even more important for our happiness than freedom to spend our income during our hours of leisure.

Even in the best of worlds this freedom will be limited. Few people ever have an abundance of choice of occupation. But what matters is that we have some choice, that we are not absolutely tied to a job which has been chosen for us, and that if one position becomes intolerable, or if we set our heart on another, there is always a way for the able, at some sacrifice, to achieve his goal. Nothing makes conditions more unbearable than the knowledge that no effort of ours can change them. It may be bad to be just a cog in a machine but it is infinitely worse if we can no longer leave it, if we are tied to our place and to the superiors who have been chosen for us.

In our present world there is much that could be done to improve our opportunities of choice. But 'planning' would surely go in the opposite direction. Planning must control the entry into the different trades and occupations, or the terms of remuneration, or both. In almost all known instances of planning, the establishment of such controls and restrictions was among the first measures taken.

In a competitive society most things can be had at a price. It is often a cruelly high price. We must sacrifice one thing to attain another. The alternative, however, is not freedom of choice, but orders and prohibitions which must be obeyed.

That people should wish to be relieved of the bitter choice which hard facts often impose on them is not surprising. But few want to be relieved through having the choice made for them by others. People just wish that the choice should not be necessary at all. And they are only too ready to believe that the choice is not really necessary, that it is imposed upon them merely by the particular economic system under which we live. What they resent is, in truth, that there is an economic problem.

The wishful delusion that there is really no longer an economic problem has been furthered by the claim that a planned economy would produce a substantially larger output than the competitive system. This claim, however, is being progressively abandoned by most students of the problem. Even a good many economists with socialist views are now content to hope that a planned society will equal the efficiency of a competitive system. They advocate planning because it will enable us to secure a more equitable distribution of wealth. And it is indisputable that, if we want consciously to decide who is to have what, we must plan the whole economic system.

But the question remains whether the price we should have to pay for the realization of somebody's ideal of justice is not bound to be more discontent and more oppression than was ever caused by the much abused free play of economic forces.

For when a government undertakes to distribute the wealth, by what principles will it or ought it to be guided? Is there a definite answer to the innumerable questions of relative merits that will arise?

Only one general principle, one simple rule, would provide such an answer: absolute equality of all individuals. If this were the goal, it would at least give the vague idea of distributive justice clear meaning. But people in general do not regard mechanical equality of this kind as desirable, and socialism promises not complete equality but 'greater equality'.

This formula answers practically no questions. It does not free us from the necessity of deciding in every particular instance between the merits of particular individuals or groups, and it gives no help in that decision. All it tells us in effect is to take from the rich as much as we can. When it comes to the distribution of the spoils the problem is the same as if the formula of 'greater equality' had never been conceived.

It is often said that political freedom is meaningless without economic freedom. This is true enough, but in a sense almost opposite from that in which the phrase is used by our planners. The economic freedom which is the prerequisite of any other freedom cannot be the freedom from economic care which the socialists promise us and which can be obtained only by relieving us of the power of choice. It must be that freedom of economic activity which, together with the right of choice, carries also the risk and responsibility of that right.

Two kinds of security

Like the spurious 'economic freedom', and with more justice, economic security is often represented as an indispensable condition of real liberty. In a sense this is both true and important. Independence of mind or strength of character is rarely found among those who cannot be confident that they will make their way by their own effort.

But there are two kinds of security: the certainty of a given minimum of sustenance for all and the security of a given standard of life, of the relative position which one person or group enjoys compared with others.

There is no reason why, in a society which has reached the

general level of wealth ours has, the first kind of security should not be guaranteed to all without endangering general freedom; that is: some minimum of food, shelter and clothing, sufficient to preserve health. Nor is there any reason why the state should not help to organize a comprehensive system of social insurance in providing for those common hazards of life against which few can make adequate provision.

It is planning for security of the second kind which has such an insidious effect on liberty. It is planning designed to protect individuals or groups against diminutions of their incomes.

If, as has become increasingly true, the members of each trade in which conditions improve are allowed to exclude others in order to secure to themselves the full gain in the form of higher wages or profits, those in the trades where demand has fallen off have nowhere to go, and every change results in large unemployment. There can be little doubt that it is largely a consequence of the striving for security by these means in the last decades that unemployment and thus insecurity have so much increased.

The utter hopelessness of the position of those who, in a society which has thus grown rigid, are left outside the range of sheltered occupation can be appreciated only by those who have experienced it. There has never been a more cruel exploitation of one class by another than that of the less fortunate members of a group of producers by the well-established. This has been made possible by the 'regulation' of competition. Few catchwords have done so much harm as the ideal of a 'stabilization' of particular prices or wages, which, while securing the income of some, makes the position of the rest more and more precarious.

In England and America special privileges, especially in the form of the 'regulation' of competition, the 'stabilization' of particular prices and wages, have assumed increasing importance. With every grant of such security to one group the insecurity of the rest necessarily increases. If you guarantee to some a fixed part of a variable cake, the share left to the rest is bound to fluctuate proportionally more than the size of the whole. And the essential element of security which the competitive system offers, the great variety of opportunities, is more and more reduced.

The general endeavour to achieve security by restrictive measures, supported by the state, has in the course of time produced a progressive transformation of society – a transformation in which, as in so many other ways, Germany has led and the other countries have followed. This development has been hastened by another effect of socialist teaching, the deliberate disparagement of all activities involving economic risk and the moral opprobrium cast on the gains which make risks worth taking but which only few can win.

We cannot blame our young men when they prefer the safe, salaried position to the risk of enterprise after they have heard from their earliest youth the former described as the superior, more unselfish and disinterested occupation. The younger generation of today has grown up in a world in which, in school and press, the spirit of commercial enterprise has been represented as disreputable and the making of profit as immoral, where to employ 100 people is represented as exploitation but to command the same number as honourable.

Older people may regard this as exaggeration, but the daily experience of the university teacher leaves little doubt that, as a result of anti-capitalist propaganda, values have already altered far in advance of the change in institutions which has so far taken place. The question is whether, by changing our institutions to satisfy the new demands, we shall not unwittingly destroy values which we still rate higher.

The conflict with which we have to deal is a fundamental one between two irreconcilable types of social organization, which have often been described as the commercial and the military. In either both choice and risk rest with the individual or he is relieved of both. In the army, work and worker alike are allotted by authority, and this is the only system in which the individual can be conceded full economic security. This security is, however, inseparable from the restrictions on liberty and the hierarchical order of military life – it is the security of the barracks.

In a society used to freedom it is unlikely that many people would be ready deliberately to purchase security at this price. But the policies which are followed now are nevertheless rapidly creating conditions in which the striving for security tends to become stronger than the love of freedom.

If we are not to destroy individual freedom, competition must be left to function unobstructed. Let a uniform minimum be secured to everybody by all means; but let us admit at the same time that all claims for a privileged security of particular classes must lapse, that all excuses disappear for allowing particular groups to exclude newcomers from sharing their relative prosperity in order to maintain a special standard of their own.

There can be no question that adequate security against severe privation will have to be one of our main goals of policy. But nothing is more fatal than the present fashion of intellectual leaders of extolling security at the expense of freedom. It is essential that we should re-learn frankly to face the fact that freedom can be had only at a price and that as individuals we must be prepared to make severe material sacrifices to preserve it.

We must regain the conviction on which liberty in the Anglo-Saxon countries has been based and which Benjamin Franklin expressed in a phrase applicable to us as individuals no less than as nations: 'Those who would give up essential liberty to purchase a little temporary safety deserve neither liberty nor safety.'

Toward a better world

To build a better world, we must have the courage to make a new start. We must clear away the obstacles with which human folly has recently encumbered our path and release the creative energy of individuals. We must create conditions favourable to progress rather than 'planning progress'.

It is not those who cry for more 'planning' who show the necessary courage, nor those who preach a 'New Order', which is no more than a continuation of the tendencies of the past 40 years, and who can think of nothing better than to imitate Hitler. It is, indeed, those who cry loudest for a planned economy who are most completely under the sway of the ideas which have created this war and most of the evils from which we suffer.

The guiding principle in any attempt to create a world of free men must be this: a policy of freedom for the individual is the only truly progressive policy.

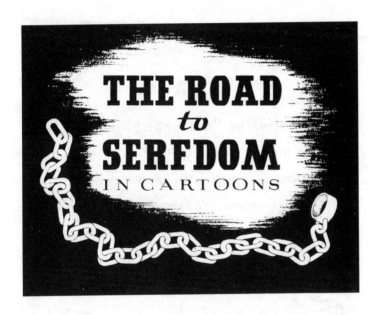

Originally published in *Look* magazine

Reproduced from a booklet published by
General Motors, Detroit, in the 'Thought Starter' series (no. 118)

THE ROAD TO SERFDOM

❶

War forces "national planning"

To permit total mobilization of your country's economy, you gladly surrender many freedoms. You know regimentation was forced by your country's enemies.

THE   ROAD   TO   SERFDOM

Many want "planning" to stay . . .

Arguments for a "peace production board" are heard before the war ends. Wartime "planners" who want to stay in power, encourage the idea.

WHAT'S GOOD IN WAR IS GOOD IN PEACE

THE ROAD TO SERFDOM

3

The "Planners" promise Utopias . . . .

A rosy plan for farmers goes well in rural areas, a plan for industrial workers is popular in cities—and so on. Many new "planners" are elected to office

→

THE ROAD TO SERFDOM

but they can't agree on ONE Utopia

With peace, a new legislature meets; but "win the war" unity is gone. The "planners" nearly come to blows. Each has his own pet plan, won't budge.

THE ROAD TO SERFDOM

5

And citizens can't agree either . . . .

When the "planners" finally patch up a temporary plan months later, citizens in turn disagree. What the farmer likes, the factory worker doesn't like.

THE ROAD TO SERFDOM

"Planners" hate to force agreement . . .

Most "national planners" are well-mean-ing idealists, balk at any use of force. They hope for some miracle of public agreement as to their patchwork plan.

T H E   R O A D   T O   S E R F D O M

7

They try to "sell" the plan to all . . .

In an unsuccessful effort to educate people to uniform views, "planners" establish a giant propaganda machine —which coming dictator will find handy.

THE ROAD TO SERFDOM

The gullible do find agreement . . . .

Meanwhile, growing national confusion leads to protest meetings. The least educated—thrilled and convinced by fiery oratory, form a party.

THE   ROAD   TO   SERFDOM

9

Confidence in "planners" fades . . . .

The more that the "planners" improvise, the greater the disturbance to normal business. Everybody suffers. People now feel—rightly—that "planners" *can't get things done!*

THE ROAD TO SERFDOM

The "strong man" is given power . . .

In desperation, "planners" authorize the
new party leader to hammer out a plan
and force its obedience. Later, they'll
dispense with him—*or so they think.*

T H E   R O A D   T O   S E R F D O M

The party takes over the country . . .

By now, confusion is so great that
obedience to the new leader must be
obtained at all costs. Maybe you join
the party yourself to aid national unity.

THE ROAD TO SERFDOM

A *negative* aim welds party unity . . .

Early step of all dictators is to inflame the majority in common cause against some scapegoat minority. In Germany, the negative aim was *Anti-Semitism.*

THE ROAD TO SERFDOM

13

No one opposes the leader's plan . . .

It would be suicide; new secret police are ruthless. Ability to force obedience always becomes the No. 1 virtue in the "planned state." Now *all* freedom is gone.

THE ROAD TO SERFDOM

Your profession is "planned" . . . .

The wider job choice promised by now defunct "planners" turns out to be a tragic farce. "Planners" never have delivered, never will be able to.

THE   ROAD   TO   SERFDOM

Your wages are "planned" . . . .
Divisions of the wage scale must
be arbitrary and rigid. Running a
"planned state" from central head-
quarters is *clumsy, unfair, inefficient.*

THE ROAD TO SERFDOM

Your thinking is "planned" . . . .
In the dictatorship, unintentionally created by the planners, there is no room for difference of opinion. Posters, radio, press—*all tell you the same lies!*

THE ROAD TO SERFDOM

Your recreation is "planned" . . . .
It is no coincidence that sports and amusements have been carefully "planned" in all regimented nations. Once started, "planners" can't stop.

THE ROAD TO SERFDOM

Your disciplining is "planned" . . . .

If you're fired from your job, it's apt to be by a firing squad. What used to be an *error* has now become a *crime* against the state. ***Thus ends the road to serfdom!***

The Intellectuals and Socialism

A note on the text

'The Intellectuals and Socialism' was first published in the *University of Chicago Law Review*, Vol. 16, No. 3, Spring 1949. It was reprinted in F. A. Hayek, *Studies in Philosophy, Politics and Economics*, Routledge and Kegan Paul, London, 1967. It was published as a booklet in the Studies in Social Theory Series by the Institute of Humane Studies, California, 1971. The text of this edition is taken from *Studies in Philosophy, Politics and Economics*. The copyright of 'The Intellectuals and Socialism' remains with the University of Chicago Law Review, and the essay is republished here by kind permission. This essay was also previously published by the IEA in the Rediscovered Riches series.

FOREWORD

In the late Professor F. A. Hayek's 1949 essay, 'The Intellectuals and Socialism', the author's final paragraph warns: 'Unless we can make the philosophic foundations of a free society once more a living intellectual issue, and its implementation a task which challenges the ingenuity and imagination of our liveliest minds, the prospects of freedom are indeed dark. But if we can regain that belief in the power of ideas which was the mark of liberalism at its best, the battle is not lost. The intellectual revival of liberalism is already under way in many parts of the world. Will it be in time?'

Fortunately, Professor Hayek's warning was heeded, just in time. His colleagues in the Mont Pèlerin Society, his students, and his admirers from around the world took his message to heart, and they have spent the decades since the publication of this essay honing their arguments for liberty, and transmitting these ideas through institutions, publications and conferences with a success undreamt of in 1949.

For many of us, Hayek's brief essay was a call to action. In it, he explained the process by which ideas are developed and become widely accepted, and he noted why our own classical liberal ideas may not be as widely held, or as fashionable, as they deserve to be. For too long we had underestimated the power of the 'intellectual class' – the 'professional second-hand dealers in ideas', as Hayek refers to them – to shape the climate of public opinion. As Hayek pointed out, the parties of the Left directed most of their energies, either by design or circumstance, toward gaining the support of this intellectual elite – the journalists, teachers, ministers, lecturers, publicists, writers, and artists who were masters of the technique of conveying ideas. At the time of this essay Hayek said that most of us learn little about events or ideas except through this class (and with the growth of television, it's probably even less). The intellectuals have become gatekeepers for the information, views, and opinions that ultimately do reach us. Conservatives, by contrast, had concentrated on reaching and persuading individual voters.

For many of us, this essay was a challenge to build up our own class of intellectuals made up of those who loved liberty. We trained, hired, networked, and supported academics, policy analysts, journalists, radio talk show hosts, and even political leaders who would shape public opinion and influence the politics of tomorrow. And in many areas we have succeeded in changing the climate of public opinion *and* changing the world. Communism has failed, the Berlin Wall has been torn down, and even left-of-centre politicians like [former] President Clinton and Prime Minister Blair are embracing the rhetoric of our classical liberal solutions when talking of some of our modern social problems. I believe the irony would not be lost on Professor Hayek!

Clearly much remains to be done before we can enjoy a truly free society. And for guidance we should once again turn to Hayek. As he points out, much of the success socialism gained up until 1949 was not by engaging in a battle of conflicting ideals, but by contrasting the existing state of affairs with that one ideal of a possible future society which the socialists alone held up before the public. 'Very few of the other programmes which offered themselves provided genuine alternatives.' (p. 123.) Compromises were thus made somewhere between the socialist ideal and the existing state of affairs. The only questions for socialists were how fast and how far to proceed. Conservatives have learned this lesson: it is not enough to stop bad policies, we have to offer genuine alternatives.

Since the original publication of 'The Intellectuals and Socialism' we have developed the philosophical foundations of a free society, thanks to Hayek, our friends at the IEA, and others. And we have built a class of intellectuals to translate these philosophical ideas to the public. However, we have not held up before the public our own vision of a future society built on liberty. And this is the task facing us as we approach the new millennium. As Hayek said, the task of constructing a free society can be exciting and fascinating. If we are to succeed, we must make the building of a free society once more an intellectual adventure and a deed of courage.

As an *alumnus* of the Institute of Economic Affairs, I particularly thank our good friends at the IEA for republishing this very special essay, and most importantly for the many courageous intellectual adventures they have undertaken.

EDWIN J. FEULNER JR

INTRODUCTION
Hayek and the Second-hand Dealers in Ideas

In April 1945 *Reader's Digest* published the condensed version of Friedrich Hayek's classic work *The Road to Serfdom.* For the first and still the only time in the history of the *Digest,* the condensed book was carried at the front of the magazine rather than the back.

Among the many who read the condensed book was Antony Fisher. In his very early thirties, this former Battle of Britain pilot turned stockbroker turned farmer went to see Hayek at the London School of Economics to discuss his concern over the advance of socialism and collectivism in Britain. Fisher feared that the country for whom so many, including his father and brother, had died in two world wars in order that it should remain free was, in fact, becoming less and less free. He saw liberty threatened by the ever-growing power and scope of the state. The purpose of his visit to Hayek, the great architect of the revival of classical liberal ideas, was to ask what could be done about it.

> My central question was what, if anything, could he advise
> me to do to help get discussion and policy on the right lines
> … Hayek first warned me against wasting time – as I was
> then tempted – by taking up a political career. He explained
> his view that the decisive influence in the battle of ideas and
> policy was wielded by intellectuals whom he characterised
> as the 'second-hand dealers in ideas'. It was the dominant
> intellectuals from the Fabians onwards who had tilted
> the political debate in favour of growing government

intervention with all that followed. If I shared the view that better ideas were not getting a fair hearing, his counsel was that I should join with others in forming a scholarly research organisation to supply intellectuals in universities, schools, journalism and broadcasting with authoritative studies of the economic theory of markets and its application to practical affairs.[1]

Fisher went on to make his fortune by introducing factory farming of chickens on the American model to Britain. His company, Buxted Chickens, changed the diet of his fellow countrymen, and made him rich enough to carry out Hayek's advice. He set up the Institute of Economic Affairs in 1955 with the view that:

> [T]hose carrying on intellectual work must have a considerable impact through newspapers, radio, television and so on, on the thinking of the average individual. *Socialism was spread in this way and it is time we started to reverse the process.*[2]

He thus set himself exactly the task which Hayek had recommended to him in 1945.

Soon after that meeting with Fisher, Hayek expanded on his theory of the influence of intellectuals in an essay entitled 'The Intellectuals and Socialism', first published in the *Chicago Law Review* in 1949 and now republished by the Institute of Economic Affairs.

---

1   A. Fisher, *Must History Repeat Itself?*, Churchill Press, 1974, p. 103, quoted in R. Cockett, *Thinking the Unthinkable*, HarperCollins, London, 1995, pp. 123–4.

2   Letter from Antony Fisher to Oliver Smedley, 22 May 1956, quoted in R. Cockett, op. cit., p. 131. Emphasis in original.

According to Hayek, the intellectual is neither an original thinker nor an expert. Indeed he need not even be intelligent. What he does possess is:

a) the ability to speak/write on a wide range of subjects; and
b) a way of becoming familiar with new ideas earlier than his audience.

Let me attempt to summarise Hayek's insights:

1. Pro-market ideas had failed to remain relevant and inspiring, thus opening the door to anti-market forces.
2. People's knowledge of history plays a much greater role in the development of their political philosophy than we normally think.[3]
3. Practical men and women concerned with the minutiae of today's events tend to lose sight of long-term considerations.
4. Be alert to special interests, especially those that, while claiming to be pro-free enterprise in general, always want to make exceptions in their own areas of expertise.
5. The outcome of today's politics is already set, so look for leverage for tomorrow as a scholar or intellectual.
6. The intellectual is the gatekeeper of ideas.
7. The best pro-market people become businessmen, engineers, doctors and so on; the best anti-market people become intellectuals and scholars.
8. Be Utopian and believe in the power of ideas.

---

3   As Leonard P. Liggio, executive vice president of the Atlas Economic Research Foundation, often says, more people learn their economics from history than from economics.

Hayek's primary example is the period 1850 to 1950, during which socialism was nowhere, at first, a working-class movement. There was always a long-term effort by the intellectuals before the working classes accepted socialism. Indeed all countries that have turned to socialism experienced an earlier phase in which for many years socialist ideas governed the thinking of more active intellectuals. Once you reach this phase, experience suggests, it is just a matter of time before the views of today's intellectuals become tomorrow's politics.

'The Intellectuals and Socialism' was published in 1949, but, apart from one reference in one sentence, there is nothing to say it could not have been written forty years later, just before Hayek's death. It might have been written forty years earlier but for the fact that, as a young man, he felt the over-generous instincts of socialism. When Hayek penned his thoughts, socialism seemed triumphant across the world. Anybody of enlightened sensibility regarded themselves as of 'The Left'. To be of 'The Right' was to be morally deformed, foolish, or both.

In Alan Bennett's 1968 play *Forty Years On* the headmaster of Albion House, a minor public school which represents Britain, asks: 'Why is it always the intelligent people who are socialists?'[4] Hayek's answer, which he expressed in his last major work, *The Fatal Conceit*, was that 'intelligent people will tend to overvalue intelligence'. They think that everything worth knowing can be discovered by processes of intellectual examination and 'find it hard to believe that there can exist any useful knowledge that did not originate in deliberate experimentation'. They consequently

---

4   A. Bennett, *Forty Years On*, first performance 31 October 1968; Faber and Faber, London, 1969, p. 58.

neglect the 'traditional rules', the 'second endowment' of 'cultural evolution' which, for Hayek, included morals, especially 'our institutions of property, freedom and justice'. They think that any imperfection can be corrected by 'rational coordination' and this leads them 'to be favourably disposed to the central economic planning and control that lie at the heart of socialism'. Thus, whether or not they call themselves socialists, 'the higher we climb up the ladder of intelligence ... the more likely we are to encounter socialist convictions'.[5]

Only when you start to list all the different groups of intellectuals do you realise how many there are, how their role has grown in modern times, and how dependent we have become on them. The more obvious ones are those who are professionals at conveying a message but are amateurs when it comes to substance. They include the 'journalists, teachers, ministers, lecturers, publicists, radio commentators, writers of fiction, cartoonists, and artists'. However we should also note the role of 'professional men and technicians' (p. 107) who are listened to by others with respect on topics outside their competence because of their standing. The intellectuals decide what we hear, in what form we are to hear it and from what angle it is to be presented. They decide who will be heard and who will not be heard. The supremacy and pervasiveness of television as the controlling medium of modern culture makes that even more true of our own day than it was in the 1940s.

There is an alarming sentence in this essay: '[I]n most parts of the Western World even the most determined opponents of

---

5   F. Hayek, *The Fatal Conceit: The Errors of Socialism*, in W. W. Bartley (ed.), *The Collected Works of Friedrich August Hayek*, Routledge, London, Vol. 1, 1988, pp. 52–4.

socialism derive from socialist sources their knowledge on most subjects on which they have no first-hand information' (p. 112). Division of knowledge is a part of the division of labour. Knowledge, and its manipulation, are the bulk of much labour now. A majority earns its living in services of myriad sorts rather than in manufacturing or agriculture.

A liberal, or as Hayek would always say, a Whig, cannot disagree with a socialist analysis in a field in which he has no knowledge. The disquieting theme of Hayek's argument is how the fragmentation of knowledge is a tactical boon to socialists. Experts in particular fields often gain 'rents' from state intervention and, while overtly free-market in their outlook elsewhere, are always quick to explain why the market does not work in their area.

This was one of the reasons for establishing the IEA and its 100-plus sister bodies around the world. Hayek also regarded the creation of the Mont Pèlerin Society, which first met in 1947, as an opportunity for minds engaged in the fight against socialism to exchange ideas – meaning, by socialism, all those ideas devoted to empowering the state. The threat posed by the forces of coercion to those of voluntary association or spontaneous action is what concerned him.

The struggle has become more difficult as policy makers have become less and less willing to identify themselves explicitly as socialists. A review of a book on socialism which appeared in 1885 began:

> Socialism is the hobby of the day. Platform and study resound with the word, and street and debating society inscribe it on their banners.[6]

---

6   Review of *Contemporary Socialism* by John Rae, *Charity Organisation Review*, Charity Organisation Society, London, October 1885.

How unlike the home life of our own New Labour! Socialism has become the 's' word, and was not mentioned in the Labour Party's 1997 election manifesto.[7]

Socialism survives, however, by transmuting itself into new forms. State-run enterprises are now frowned upon, but the ever-expanding volume of regulation – financial, environmental, health and safety – serves to empower the state by other means.

Part of Hayek's charm is the pull of his sheer geniality. He is generous and mannerly in acknowledging that most socialists have benign intentions. They are blind to the real flaws of their recipes. Typically, Hayek ends with a point in their favour: '[I]t was their courage to be Utopian which gained them the support of the intellectuals and therefore an influence on public opinion' (p. 129). Those who concern themselves exclusively with what seems practicable are marginalised by the greater influence of prevailing opinion.

I commend to you Hayek's urge not to seek compromises. We can leave that to the politicians. 'Free trade and freedom of opportunity are ideals which still may arouse the imaginations of large numbers, but a mere "reasonable freedom of trade" or a mere "relaxation of controls" is neither intellectually respectable nor likely to inspire any enthusiasm' (p. 129).

Most of the readers of this paper will be Hayek's 'second-hand dealers in ideas'. Conceit makes us all prone to believe we are original thinkers, but Hayek explains that we are mostly transmitters of ideas borrowed from earlier minds (hence second-hand, in

---

7   *New Labour: Because Britain Deserves Better*, The Labour Party, London, 1997. On the contrary, the manifesto complained that: 'Our system of government is centralised, inefficient and bureaucratic.'

a non-pejorative sense). Those scholars who really are the founts of new ideas are far more rare than we all suppose. However, Hayek argues that we, and the world, are governed by ideas and that we can only expand our political and policy horizons by deploying them.

He was supported in this view – and it was probably the only view they shared – by John Maynard Keynes. In 1936 Keynes had concluded his most famous book, *The General Theory of Employment, Interest and Money*, with these ringing words:

> … the ideas of economists and political philosophers, both when they are right and when they are wrong, are more powerful than is commonly understood. Indeed the world is ruled by little else. Practical men, who believe themselves to be quite exempt from any intellectual influences, are usually the slaves of some defunct economist … Soon or late, it is ideas, not vested interests, which are dangerous for good or evil.[8]

Of course, this was true of no one more than of Keynes himself, whose followers were wreaking havoc with the world's economies long after he had become defunct. But it was also true of Hayek. It was Hayek's great good fortune to live long enough to see his own ideas enter the mainstream of public policy debate. They were not always attributed to him: they were described as Thatcherism, or Adam-Smith liberalism, or neo-conservatism, but he was responsible for their re-emergence, whether credited or not. We received a striking demonstration of this at the IEA in 1996 when we invited Donald Brash, the Governor of the Reserve Bank

---

8   J. M. Keynes, *The General Theory of Employment, Interest and Money*, Macmillan, London, p. 383.

of New Zealand, to give the prestigious Annual Hayek Memorial Lecture on the subject of 'New Zealand's Remarkable Reforms'. He admitted that, although 'the New Zealand reforms have a distinctly Hayekian flavour', the architects of them were scarcely aware of Hayek at all, and Brash himself had never read a word of Hayek before being asked to give the lecture.[9]

The IEA can claim some victories in the increasing awareness of classical liberal ideas and ideals. It is hard to measure our influence, yet, if we awaken some young scholar to the possibility that the paradigms or conventions of a discipline may be flawed, we can change the life of that mind for ever. If we convince a young journalist he can do more good, and have more fun, by criticising the remnants of our socialist inheritance, we can change that life. If we persuade a young politician he can harass the forces of inertia by tackling privilege and bureaucracy, we change the course of that life too. The IEA continues in its mission to move around the furniture in the minds of intellectuals. That includes you, probably.

JOHN BLUNDELL

9   D. T. Brash, *New Zealand's Remarkable Reforms,* Occasional Paper 100, Institute of
     Economic Affairs, London, 1996, p. 17.

THE INTELLECTUALS AND SOCIALISM

I

In all democratic countries, in the United States even more than elsewhere, a strong belief prevails that the influence of the intellectuals on politics is negligible. This is no doubt true of the power of intellectuals to make their peculiar opinions of the moment influence decisions, of the extent to which they can sway the popular vote on questions on which they differ from the current views of the masses. Yet over somewhat longer periods they have probably never exercised so great an influence as they do today in those countries. This power they wield by shaping public opinion.

In the light of recent history it is somewhat curious that this decisive power of the professional second-hand dealers in ideas should not yet be more generally recognised. The political development of the Western world during the last hundred years furnishes the clearest demonstration. Socialism has never and nowhere been at first a working-class movement. It is by no means an obvious remedy for the obvious evil which the interests of that class will necessarily demand. It is a construction of theorists, deriving from certain tendencies of abstract thought with which for a long time only the intellectuals were familiar; and it required long efforts by the intellectuals before the working classes could be persuaded to adopt it as their programme.

In every country that has moved toward socialism, the phase of the development in which socialism becomes a determining influence on politics has been preceded for many years by a period during which socialist ideals governed the thinking of the more active intellectuals. In Germany this stage had been reached towards the end of the last century; in England and France, about the time of World War I. To the casual observer it would seem as if the United States had reached this phase after World War II and that the attraction of a planned and directed economic system is now as strong among the American intellectuals as it ever was among their German or English fellows. Experience suggests that, once this phase has been reached, it is merely a question of time until the views now held by the intellectuals become the governing force of politics.

The character of the process by which the views of the intellectuals influence the politics of tomorrow is therefore of much more than academic interest. Whether we merely wish to foresee or attempt to influence the course of events, it is a factor of much greater importance than is generally understood. What to the contemporary observer appears as the battle of conflicting interests has indeed often been decided long before in a clash of ideas confined to narrow circles. Paradoxically enough, however, in general the parties of the Left have done most to spread the belief that it was the numerical strength of the opposing material interests which decided political issues, whereas in practice these same parties have regularly and successfully acted as if they understood the key position of the intellectuals. Whether by design or driven by the force of circumstances, they have always directed their main effort towards gaining the support of this 'elite', while the more conservative groups have acted, as regularly but unsuccessfully, on a more naïve view of mass democracy and have usually vainly tried directly to reach and to persuade the individual voter.

II

The term 'intellectuals', however, does not at once convey a true picture of the large class to which we refer, and the fact that we have no better name by which to describe what we have called the second-hand dealers in ideas is not the least of the reasons why their power is not better understood. Even persons who use the word 'intellectual' mainly as a term of abuse are still inclined to withhold it from many who undoubtedly perform that characteristic function. This is neither that of the original thinker nor that of the scholar or expert in a particular field of thought. The typical intellectual need be neither: he need not possess special knowledge of anything in particular, nor need he even be particularly intelligent, to perform his role as intermediary in the spreading of ideas. What qualifies him for his job is the wide range of subjects on which he can readily talk and write, and a position or habits through which he becomes acquainted with new ideas sooner than those to whom he addresses himself.

Until one begins to list all the professions and activities which belong to this class, it is difficult to realise how numerous it is, how the scope for its activities constantly increases in modern society, and how dependent on it we all have become. The class does not consist only of journalists, teachers, ministers, lecturers, publicists, radio commentators, writers of fiction, cartoonists, and artists – all of whom may be masters of the technique of conveying ideas but are usually amateurs so far as the substance of what they convey is concerned. The class also includes many professional men and technicians, such as scientists and doctors, who through their habitual intercourse with the printed word become carriers of new ideas outside their own fields and who, because of their expert knowledge of their own subjects, are listened to with respect on most others. There is little that the ordinary man of today learns about events or ideas except through the medium of this class; and outside our special fields of work we are in this respect almost all ordinary men, dependent for our information and instruction on those who make it their job to keep abreast of opinion. It is the intellectuals in this sense who decide what views and opinions are to reach us, which facts are important enough to be told to us, and in what form and from what angle they are to be presented. Whether we shall ever learn of the results of the work of the expert and the original thinker depends mainly on their decision.

The layman, perhaps, is not fully aware to what extent even the popular reputations of scientists and scholars are made by that class and are inevitably affected by its views on subjects which have little to do with the merits of the real achievements. And it is specially significant for our problem that every scholar can probably name several instances from his field of men who have undeservedly achieved a popular reputation as great scientists solely because they hold what the intellectuals regard as 'progressive' political views; but I have yet to come across a single instance where such a scientific pseudo-reputation has been bestowed for political reason on a scholar of more conservative leanings. This creation of reputations by the intellectuals is particularly important in the fields where the results of expert studies are not used by other specialists but depend on the political decision of the public at large. There is indeed scarcely a better illustration of this than the attitude which professional economists have taken to the growth of such doctrines as socialism or protectionism. There was probably at no time a majority of economists, who were recognised as such by their peers, favourable to socialism (or, for that matter, to protection). In all probability it is even true to say that no other similar group of students contains so high a proportion of its members decidedly opposed to socialism (or protection). This is the more significant as in recent times it is as likely as not that it was an early interest in socialist schemes for reform which led a man to choose economics for his profession. Yet it is not the predominant views of the experts but the views of a minority, mostly of rather doubtful standing in their profession, which are taken up and spread by the intellectuals.

The all-pervasive influence of the intellectuals in contemporary society is still further strengthened by the growing importance of 'organisation'. It is a common but probably mistaken belief that the increase of organisation increases the influence of the expert or specialist. This may be true of the expert administrator and organiser, if there are such people, but hardly of the expert in any particular field of knowledge. It is rather the person whose general knowledge is supposed to qualify him to appreciate expert testimony, and to judge between the experts from different fields, whose power is enhanced. The point which is important for us, however, is that the scholar who becomes a university president, the scientist who takes charge of an institute or foundation, the scholar who becomes an editor or the active promoter of an organisation serving a particular cause, all rapidly cease to be scholars or experts and become intellectuals in our sense, people who judge all issues not by their specific merits but, in the characteristic manner of intellectuals, solely in the light of certain fashionable general ideas. The number of such institutions which breed intellectuals and increase their number and powers grows every day. Almost all the 'experts' in the mere technique of getting knowledge over are, with respect to the subject matter which they handle, intellectuals and not experts.

In the sense in which we are using the term, the intellectuals are in fact a fairly new phenomenon of history. Though nobody will regret that education has ceased to be a privilege of the propertied classes, the fact that the propertied classes are no longer the best educated and the fact that the large number of people who owe their position solely to their general education do not possess that experience of the working of the economic system which the administration of property gives, are important for understanding the role of the intellectual. Professor Schumpeter, who has devoted an illuminating chapter of his *Capitalism, Socialism, and Democracy* to some aspects of our problem, has not unfairly stressed that it is the absence of direct responsibility for practical affairs and the consequent absence of first-hand knowledge of them which distinguishes the typical intellectual from other people who also wield the power of the spoken and written word. It would lead too far, however, to examine here further the development of this class and the curious claim which has recently been advanced by one of its theorists that it was the only one whose views were not decidedly influenced by its own economic interests. One of the important points that would have to be examined in such a discussion would be how far the growth of this class has been artificially stimulated by the law of copyright.[1]

---

1   It would be interesting to discover how far a seriously critical view of the benefits to society of the law of copyright, or the expression of doubts about the public interest in the existence of a class which makes its living from the writing of books, would have a chance of being publicly stated in a society in which the channels of expression are so largely controlled by people who have a vested interest in the existing situation.

III

It is not surprising that the real scholar or expert and the practical man of affairs often feel contemptuous about the intellectual, are disinclined to recognise his power, and are resentful when they discover it. Individually they find the intellectuals mostly to be people who understand nothing in particular especially well and whose judgement on matters they themselves understand shows little sign of special wisdom. But it would be a fatal mistake to underestimate their power for this reason. Even though their knowledge may be often superficial and their intelligence limited, this does not alter the fact that it is their judgement which mainly determines the views on which society will act in the not too distant future. It is no exaggeration to say that, once the more active part of the intellectuals has been converted to a set of beliefs, the process by which these become generally accepted is almost automatic and irresistible. These intellectuals are the organs which modern society has developed for spreading knowledge and ideas, and it is their convictions and opinions which operate as the sieve through which all new conceptions must pass before they can reach the masses.

It is of the nature of the intellectual's job that he must use his own knowledge and convictions in performing his daily task. He occupies his position because he possesses, or has had to deal from day to day with, knowledge which his employer in general does not possess, and his activities can therefore be directed by others only to a limited extent. And just because the intellectuals are mostly intellectually honest, it is inevitable that they should follow their own convictions whenever they have discretion and that they should give a corresponding slant to everything that passes through their hands. Even where the direction of policy is in the hands of men of affairs of different views, the execution of policy will in general be in the hands of intellectuals, and it is frequently the decision on the detail which determines the net effect. We find this illustrated in almost all fields of contemporary society. Newspapers in 'capitalist' ownership, universities presided over by 'reactionary' governing bodies, broadcasting systems owned by conservative governments, have all been known to influence public opinion in the direction of socialism, because this was the conviction of the personnel. This has often happened not only in spite of, but perhaps even because of, the attempts of those at the top to control opinion and to impose principles of orthodoxy.

The effect of this filtering of ideas through the convictions of a class which is constitutionally disposed to certain views is by no means confined to the masses. Outside his special field the expert is generally no less dependent on this class and scarcely less influenced by their selection. The result of this is that today in most parts of the Western world even the most determined opponents of socialism derive from socialist sources their knowledge on most subjects on which they have no first-hand information. With many of the more general preconceptions of socialist thought, the connection of their more practical proposals is by no means at once obvious; in consequence, many men who believe themselves to be determined opponents of that system of thought become in fact effective spreaders of its ideas. Who does not know the practical man who in his own field denounces socialism as 'pernicious rot' but, when he steps outside his subject, spouts socialism like any Left journalist?

In no other field has the predominant influence of the socialist intellectuals been felt more strongly during the last hundred years than in the contacts between different national civilisations. It would go far beyond the limits of this article to trace the causes and significance of the highly important fact that in the modern world the intellectuals provide almost the only approach to an international community. It is this which mainly accounts for the extraordinary spectacle that for generations the supposedly 'capitalist' West has been lending its moral and material support almost exclusively to those ideological movements in the countries farther east which aimed at undermining Western civilisation and that, at the same time, the information which the Western public has obtained about events in Central and Eastern Europe has almost inevitably been coloured by a socialist bias. Many of the 'educational' activities of the American forces of occupation in Germany have furnished clear and recent examples of this tendency.

IV

A proper understanding of the reasons which tend to incline so many of the intellectuals towards socialism is thus most important. The first point here which those who do not share this bias ought to face frankly is that it is neither selfish interests nor evil intentions but mostly honest convictions and good intentions which determine the intellectuals' views. In fact, it is necessary to recognise that on the whole the typical intellectual is today more likely to be a socialist the more he is guided by good will and intelligence, and that on the plane of purely intellectual argument he will generally be able to make out a better case than the majority of his opponents within his class. If we still think him wrong, we must recognise that it may be genuine error which leads the well-meaning and intelligent people who occupy those key positions in our society to spread views which to us appear a threat to our civilisation.[2] Nothing could be more important than to try to understand the sources of this error in order that we should be able to counter it. Yet those who are generally regarded as the representatives of the existing order and who believe that they comprehend the dangers of socialism are usually very far from such understanding. They tend to regard the socialist intellectuals as nothing more than a pernicious bunch of highbrow radicals without appreciating their influence and, by their whole attitude to them, tend to drive them even further into opposition to the existing order.

If we are to understand this peculiar bias of a large section of the intellectuals, we must be clear about two points. The first is that they generally judge all particular issues exclusively in the light of certain general ideas; the second, that the characteristic errors of any age are frequently derived from some genuine new truths it has discovered, and they are erroneous applications of new generalisations which have proved their value in other fields. The conclusion to which we shall be led by a full consideration of these facts will be that the effective refutation of such errors will frequently require further intellectual advance, and often advance on points which are very abstract and may seem very remote from the practical issues.

It is perhaps the most characteristic feature of the intellectual that he judges new ideas not by their specific merits but by the readiness with which they fit into his general conceptions, into the

---

2   It was therefore not (as has been suggested by one reviewer of *The Road to Serfdom*, Professor J. Schumpeter) 'politeness to a fault' but profound conviction of the importance of this which made me, in Professor Schumpeter's words, 'hardly ever attribute to opponents anything beyond intellectual error'.

picture of the world which he regards as modern or advanced. It is through their influence on him and on his choice of opinions on particular issues that the power of ideas for good and evil grows in proportion to their generality, abstractness, and even vagueness. As he knows little about the particular issues, his criterion must be consistency with his other views and suitability for combining into a coherent picture of the world. Yet this selection from the multitude of new ideas presenting themselves at every moment creates the characteristic climate of opinion, the dominant *Weltanschauung* of a period, which will be favourable to the reception of some opinions and unfavourable to others and which will make the intellectual readily accept one conclusion and reject another without a real understanding of the issues.

In some respects the intellectual is indeed closer to the philosopher than to any specialist, and the philosopher is in more than one sense a sort of prince among the intellectuals. Although his influence is farther removed from practical affairs and correspondingly slower and more difficult to trace than that of the ordinary intellectual, it is of the same kind and in the long run even more powerful than that of the latter. It is the same endeavour towards a synthesis, pursued more methodically, the same judgement of particular views in so far as they fit into a general system of thought rather than by their specific merits, the same striving after a consistent world view, which for both forms the main basis for accepting or rejecting ideas. For this reason the philosopher has probably a greater influence over the intellectuals than any other scholar or scientist and, more than anyone else, determines the manner in which the intellectuals exercise their censorship function. The popular influence of the scientific specialist begins to rival that of the philosopher only when he ceases to be a specialist and commences to philosophise about the progress of his subject – and usually only after he has been taken up by the intellectuals for reasons which have little to do with his scientific eminence.

The 'climate of opinion' of any period is thus essentially a set of very general preconceptions by which the intellectual judges the importance of new facts and opinions. These preconceptions are mainly applications to what seem to him the most significant aspects of scientific achievements, a transfer to other fields of what has particularly impressed him in the work of the specialists. One could give a long list of such intellectual fashions and catch-words which in the course of two or three generations have in turn dominated the thinking of the intellectuals. Whether it was the 'historical approach' or the theory of evolution, nineteenth-century determinism and the belief in the predominant influence of environment as against heredity, the theory of relativity or the belief in the power of the unconscious – every one of these general conceptions has been made the touchstone by which innovations in different fields have been tested. It seems as if the less specific or precise (or the less understood) these ideas are, the wider may be their influence. Sometimes it is no more than a vague impression rarely put into words which thus wields a profound influence. Such beliefs as that deliberate control or conscious organisation is also in social affairs always superior to the results of spontaneous processes which are not directed by a human mind, or that any order based on a plan laid down beforehand must be better than one formed by the balancing of opposing forces, have in this way profoundly affected political development.

Only apparently different is the role of the intellectuals where the development of more properly social ideas is concerned. Here their peculiar propensities manifest themselves in making shibboleths of abstractions, in rationalising and carrying to extremes certain ambitions which spring from the normal intercourse of men. Since democracy is a good thing, the further the democratic principle can be carried, the better it appears to them. The most powerful of these general ideas which have shaped political development in recent times is of course the ideal of material equality. It is, characteristically, not one of the spontaneously grown moral convictions, first applied in the relations between particular individuals, but an intellectual construction originally conceived in the abstract and of doubtful meaning or application in particular instances. Nevertheless, it has operated strongly as a principle of selection among the alternative courses of social policy, exercising a persistent pressure towards an arrangement of social affairs which nobody clearly conceives. That a particular measure tends to bring about greater equality has come to be regarded as so strong a recommendation that little else will be considered. Since on each particular issue it is this one aspect on which those who guide opinion have a definite conviction, equality has determined social change even more strongly than its advocates intended.

Not only moral ideals act in this manner, however. Sometimes the attitudes of the intellectuals towards the problems of social order may be the consequence of advances in purely scientific knowledge, and it is in these instances that their erroneous views on particular issues may for a time seem to have all the prestige of the latest scientific achievements behind them. It is not in itself surprising that a genuine advance of knowledge should in this manner become on occasion a source of new error. If no false conclusions followed from new generalisations, they would be final truths which would never need revision. Although as a rule such a new generalisation will merely share the false consequences

THE INTELLECTUALS AND SOCIALISM

which can be drawn from it with the views which were held before, and thus not lead to new error, it is quite likely that a new theory, just as its value is shown by the valid new conclusions to which it leads, will produce other new conclusions which further advance will show to have been erroneous. But in such an instance a false belief will appear with all the prestige of the latest scientific knowledge supporting it. Although in the particular field to which this belief applies all the scientific evidence may be against it, it will nevertheless, before the tribunal of the intellectuals and in the light of the ideas which govern their thinking, be selected as the view which is best in accord with the spirit of the time. The specialists who will thus achieve public fame and wide influence will thus not be those who have gained recognition by their peers but will often be men whom the other experts regard as cranks, amateurs, or even frauds, but who in the eyes of the general public nevertheless become the best known exponents of their subject.

In particular, there can be little doubt that the manner in which during the last hundred years man has learned to organise the forces of nature has contributed a great deal towards the creation of the belief that a similar control of the forces of society would bring comparable improvements in human conditions. That, with the application of engineering techniques, the direction of all forms of human activity according to a single coherent plan should prove to be as successful in society as it has been in innumerable engineering tasks, is too plausible a conclusion not to seduce most of those who are elated by the achievement of the natural sciences. It must indeed be admitted both that it would require powerful arguments to counter the strong presumption in favour of such a conclusion and that these arguments have not yet been adequately stated. It is not sufficient to point out the defects of particular proposals based on this kind of reasoning. The argument will not lose its force until it has been conclusively shown why what has proved so eminently successful in producing advances in so many fields should have limits to its usefulness and become positively harmful if extended beyond these limits. This is a task which has not yet been satisfactorily performed and which will have to be achieved before this particular impulse towards socialism can be removed.

This, of course, is only one of many instances where further intellectual advance is needed if the harmful ideas at present current are to be refuted and where the course which we shall travel will ultimately be decided by the discussion of very abstract issues. It is not enough for the man of affairs to be sure, from his intimate knowledge of a particular field, that the theories of socialism which are derived from more general ideas will prove impracticable. He may be perfectly right, and yet his resistance will be overwhelmed and all the sorry consequences which he foresees will follow if he is not supported by an effective refutation of the *idées mères*. So long as the intellectual gets the better of the general argument, the most valid objections to the specific issue will be brushed aside.

V

This is not the whole story, however. The forces which influence recruitment to the ranks of the intellectuals operate in the same direction and help to explain why so many of the most able among them lean towards socialism. There are of course as many differences of opinion among intellectuals as among other groups of people; but it seems to be true that it is on the whole the more active, intelligent, and original men among the intellectuals who most frequently incline towards socialism, while its opponents are often of an inferior calibre. This is true particularly during the early stages of the infiltration of socialist ideas; later, although outside intellectual circles it may still be an act of courage to profess socialist convictions, the pressure of opinion among intellectuals will often be so strongly in favour of socialism that it requires more strength and independence for a man to resist it than to join in what his fellows regard as modern views. Nobody, for instance, who is familiar with large numbers of university faculties (and from this point of view the majority of university teachers probably have to be classed as intellectuals rather than as experts) can remain oblivious to the fact that the most brilliant and successful teachers are today more likely than not to be socialists, while those who hold more conservative political views are as frequently mediocrities. This is of course by itself an important factor leading the younger generation into the socialist camp.

The socialist will, of course, see in this merely a proof that the more intelligent person is today bound to become a socialist. But this is far from being the necessary or even the most likely explanation. The main reason for this state of affairs is probably that, for the exceptionally able man who accepts the present order of society, a multitude of other avenues to influence and power are open, while to the disaffected and dissatisfied an intellectual career is the most promising path to both influence and the power to contribute to the achievement of his ideals. Even more than that: the more conservatively inclined man of first class ability will in general choose intellectual work (and the sacrifice in material reward which this choice usually entails) only if he enjoys it for its own sake. He is in consequence more likely to become an expert scholar rather than an intellectual in the specific sense of the word; while to the more radically minded the intellectual pursuit is more often than not a means rather than an end, a path to exactly that kind of wide influence which the professional intellectual exercises. It is therefore probably the fact, not that the more intelligent people are generally socialists, but that a much higher proportion of socialists among the best minds devote themselves to those intellectual pursuits which in modern society give them a decisive influence on public opinion.[3]

The selection of the personnel of the intellectuals is also closely connected with the predominant interest which they show in general and abstract ideas. Speculations about the possible entire reconstruction of society give the intellectual a fare much more to his taste than the more practical and short-run considerations of those who aim at a piecemeal improvement of the existing order. In particular, socialist thought owes its appeal to the young largely to its visionary character; the very courage to indulge in Utopian thought is in this respect a source of strength to the socialists which traditional liberalism sadly lacks. This difference operates in favour of socialism, not only because speculation about general principles provides an opportunity for the play of the imagination

---

3   Related to this is another familiar phenomenon: there is little reason to believe that really first-class intellectual ability for original work is any rarer among Gentiles than among Jews. Yet there can be little doubt that men of Jewish stock almost everywhere constitute a disproportionately large number of the intellectuals in our sense, that is of the ranks of the professional interpreters of ideas. This may be their special gift and certainly is their main opportunity in countries where prejudice puts obstacles in their way in other fields. It is probably more because they constitute so large a proportion of the intellectuals than for any other reason that they seem to be so much more receptive to socialist ideas than people of different stocks.

of those who are unencumbered by much knowledge of the facts of present-day life, but also because it satisfies a legitimate desire for the understanding of the rational basis of any social order and gives scope for the exercise of that constructive urge for which liberalism, after it had won its great victories, left few outlets. The intellectual, by his whole disposition, is uninterested in technical details or practical difficulties. What appeal to him are the broad visions, the specious comprehension of the social order as a whole which a planned system promises.

This fact that the tastes of the intellectual were better satisfied by the speculations of the socialists proved fatal to the influence of the liberal tradition. Once the basic demands of the liberal programmes seemed satisfied, the liberal thinkers turned to problems of detail and tended to neglect the development of the general philosophy of liberalism, which in consequence ceased to be a live issue offering scope for general speculation. Thus for something over half a century it has been only the socialists who have offered anything like an explicit programme of social development, a picture of the future society at which they were aiming, and a set of general principles to guide decisions on particular issues. Even though, if I am right, their ideals suffer from inherent contradictions, and any attempt to put them into practice must produce something utterly different from what they expect, this does not alter the fact that their programme for change is the only one which has actually influenced the development of social institutions. It is because theirs has become the only explicit general philosophy of social policy held by a large group, the only system or theory which raises new problems and opens new horizons, that they have succeeded in inspiring the imagination of the intellectuals.

The actual developments of society during this period were determined not by a battle of conflicting ideals, but by the contrast between an existing state of affairs and that one ideal of a possible future society which the socialists alone held up before the public. Very few of the other programmes which offered themselves provided genuine alternatives. Most of them were mere compromises or half-way houses between the more extreme types of socialism and the existing order. All that was needed to make almost any socialist proposal appear reasonable to these 'judicious' minds who were constitutionally convinced that the truth must always lie in the middle between the extremes, was for someone to advocate a sufficiently more extreme proposal. There seemed to exist only one direction in which we could move, and the only question seemed to be how fast and how far the movement should proceed.

VI

The significance of the special appeal to the intellectuals which socialism derives from its speculative character will become clearer if we further contrast the position of the socialist theorist with that of his counterpart who is a liberal in the old sense of the word. This comparison will also lead us to whatever lesson we can draw from an adequate appreciation of the intellectual forces which are undermining the foundations of a free society.

Paradoxically enough, one of the main handicaps which deprives the liberal thinker of popular influence is closely connected with the fact that, until socialism has actually arrived, he has more opportunity of directly influencing decisions on current policy and that in consequence he is not only not tempted

into that long-run speculation which is the strength of the socialists, but is actually discouraged from it because any effort of this
kind is likely to reduce the immediate good he can do. Whatever
power he has to influence practical decisions he owes to his
standing with the representatives of the existing order, and this
standing he would endanger if he devoted himself to the kind of
speculation which would appeal to the intellectuals and which
through them could influence developments over longer periods.
In order to carry weight with the powers that be, he has to be
'practical', 'sensible', and 'realistic'. So long as he concerns himself
with immediate issues, he is rewarded with influence, material
success, and popularity with those who up to a point share his
general outlook. But these men have little respect for those speculations on general principles which shape the intellectual climate.
Indeed, if he seriously indulges in such long-run speculation, he
is apt to acquire the reputation of being 'unsound' or even half a
socialist, because he is unwilling to identify the existing order with
the free system at which he aims.[4]

If, in spite of this, his efforts continue in the direction of
general speculation, he soon discovers that it is unsafe to associate
too closely with those who seem to share most of his convictions,
and he is soon driven into isolation. Indeed there can be few more

---

4   The most glaring recent example of such condemnation of a somewhat unortho-
     dox liberal work as 'socialist' has been provided by some comments on the late
     Henry Simons's *Economic Policy for a Free Society* (1948). One need not agree with
     the whole of this work and one may even regard some of the suggestions made in
     it as incompatible with a free society, and yet recognise it as one of the most im-
     portant contributions made in recent times to our problem and as just the kind of
     work which is required to get discussion started on the fundamental issues. Even
     those who violently disagree with some of its suggestions should welcome it as a
     contribution which clearly and courageously raises the central problems of our
     time.

thankless tasks at present than the essential one of developing the philosophical foundation on which the further development of a free society must be based. Since the man who undertakes it must accept much of the framework of the existing order, he will appear to many of the more speculatively minded intellectuals merely as a timid apologist of things as they are; at the same time he will be dismissed by the men of affairs as an impractical theorist. He is not radical enough for those who know only the world where 'with ease together dwell the thoughts' and much too radical for those who see only how 'hard in space together clash the things'. If he takes advantage of such support as he can get from the men of affairs, he will almost certainly discredit himself with those on whom he depends for the spreading of his ideas. At the same time he will need most carefully to avoid anything resembling extravagance or overstatement. While no socialist theorist has ever been known to discredit himself with his fellows even by the silliest of proposals, the old-fashioned liberal will damn himself by an impracticable suggestion. Yet for the intellectuals he will still not be speculative or adventurous enough, and the changes and improvements in the social structure he will have to offer will seem limited in comparison with what their less restrained imagination conceives.

At least in a society in which the main requisites of freedom have already been won and further improvements must concern points of comparative detail, the liberal programme can have none of the glamour of a new invention. The appreciation of the improvements it has to offer requires more knowledge of the working of the existing society than the average intellectual possesses. The discussion of these improvements must proceed on a more practical level than that of the more revolutionary programmes, thus giving a complexion which has little appeal for the intellectual and tending to bring in elements to whom he feels directly antagonistic. Those who are most familiar with the working of the present society are also usually interested in the preservation of particular features of that society which may not be defensible on general principles. Unlike the person who looks for an entirely new future order and who naturally turns for guidance to the theorist, the men who believe in the existing order also usually think that they understand it much better than any theorist and in consequence are likely to reject whatever is unfamiliar and theoretical.

The difficulty of finding genuine and disinterested support for a systematic policy for freedom is not new. In a passage of which the reception of a recent book of mine has often reminded me, Lord Acton long ago described how:

> at all times sincere friends of freedom have been rare, and its triumphs have been due to minorities, that have prevailed by associating themselves with auxiliaries whose objects differed from their own; and this association, which is always dangerous, has been sometimes disastrous, by giving to opponents just grounds of opposition... [5]

More recently, one of the most distinguished living American economists has complained in a similar vein that the main task of those who believe in the basic principles of the capitalist system must frequently be to defend this system against the capitalists – indeed the great liberal economists, from Adam Smith to the present, have always known this.

The most serious obstacle which separates the practical men

---

5   Acton, *The History of Freedom*, London, 1922.

who have the cause of freedom genuinely at heart from those forces which in the realm of ideas decide the course of development is their deep distrust of theoretical speculation and their tendency to orthodoxy; this, more than anything else, creates an almost impassable barrier between them and those intellectuals who are devoted to the same cause and whose assistance is indispensable if the cause is to prevail. Although this tendency is perhaps natural among men who defend a system because it has justified itself in practice, and to whom its intellectual justification seems immaterial, it is fatal to its survival because it deprives it of the support it most needs. Orthodoxy of any kind, any pretence that a system of ideas is final and must be unquestioningly accepted as a whole, is the one view which of necessity antagonises all intellectuals, whatever their views on particular issues. Any system which judges men by the completeness of their conformity to a fixed set of opinions, by their 'soundness' or the extent to which they can be relied upon to hold approved views on all points, deprives itself of a support without which no set of ideas can maintain its influence in modern society. The ability to criticise accepted views, to explore new vistas and to experiment with new conceptions, provides the atmosphere without which the intellectual cannot breathe. A cause which offers no scope for these traits can have no support from him and is thereby doomed in any society which, like ours, rests on his services.

VII

It may be that a free society as we have known it carries in itself the forces of its own destruction, that once freedom has been achieved it is taken for granted and ceases to be valued, and that the free growth of ideas which is the essence of a free society will bring about the destruction of the foundations on which it depends. There can be little doubt that in countries like the United States the ideal of freedom has today less real appeal for the young than it has in countries where they have learned what its loss means. On the other hand, there is every sign that in Germany and elsewhere, to the young men who have never known a free society, the task of constructing one can become as exciting and fascinating as any socialist scheme which has appeared during the last hundred years. It is an extraordinary fact, though one which many visitors have experienced, that in speaking to German students about the principles of a liberal society one finds a more responsive and even enthusiastic audience than one can hope to find in any of the Western democracies. In Britain also there is already appearing among the young a new interest in the principles of true liberalism which certainly did not exist a few years ago.

Does this mean that freedom is valued only when it is lost, that the world must everywhere go through a dark phase of socialist totalitarianism before the forces of freedom can gather strength anew? It may be so, but I hope it need not be. Yet, so long as the people who over longer periods determine public opinion continue to be attracted by the ideals of socialism, the trend will continue. If we are to avoid such a development, we must be able to offer a new liberal programme which appeals to the imagination. We must make the building of a free society once more an intellectual adventure, a deed of courage. What we lack is a liberal Utopia, a programme which seems neither a mere defence of things as they are nor a diluted kind of socialism, but a truly liberal radicalism which does not spare the susceptibilities of the mighty (including the trade unions), which is not too severely practical, and which does not confine itself to what appears today as politically possible. We need intellectual leaders who are prepared to resist the blandishments of power and influence and who are willing to work for an ideal, however small may be the prospects of its early realisation. They must be men who are willing to stick to principles and to fight for their full realisation, however remote. The practical compromises they must leave to the politicians. Free trade and freedom of opportunity are ideals which still may arouse the imaginations of large numbers, but a mere 'reasonable freedom of trade' or a mere 'relaxation of controls' is neither intellectually respectable nor likely to inspire any enthusiasm.

The main lesson which the true liberal must learn from the success of the socialists is that it was their courage to be Utopian which gained them the support of the intellectuals and therefore an influence on public opinion which is daily making possible what only recently seemed utterly remote. Those who have concerned themselves exclusively with what seemed practicable in the existing state of opinion have constantly found that even this has rapidly become politically impossible as the result of changes in a public opinion which they have done nothing to guide. Unless we can make the philosophic foundations of a free society once more a living intellectual issue, and its implementation a task which challenges the ingenuity and imagination of our liveliest minds, the prospects of freedom are indeed dark. But if we can regain that belief in the power of ideas which was the mark of liberalism at its best, the battle is not lost. The intellectual revival of liberalism is already under way in many parts of the world. Will it be in time?

ABOUT THE IEA

The Institute is a research and educational charity (No. CC 235 351), limited by guarantee. Its mission is to improve understanding of the fundamental institutions of a free society with particular reference to the role of markets in solving economic and social problems.

The IEA achieves its mission by:

- a high-quality publishing programme
- conferences, seminars, lectures and other events
- outreach to school and college students
- brokering media introductions and appearances

The IEA, which was established in 1955 by the late Sir Antony Fisher, is an educational charity, not a political organisation. It is independent of any political party or group and does not carry on activities intended to affect support for any political party or candidate in any election or referendum, or at any other time. It is financed by sales of publications, conference fees and voluntary donations.

In addition to its main series of publications the IEA also publishes a quarterly journal, *Economic Affairs*.

The IEA is aided in its work by a distinguished international Academic Advisory Council and an eminent panel of Honorary Fellows. Together with other academics, they review prospective IEA publications, their comments being passed on anonymously to authors. All IEA papers are therefore subject to the same rigorous independent refereeing process as used by leading academic journals.

IEA publications enjoy widespread classroom use and course adoptions in schools and universities. They are also sold throughout the world and often translated/reprinted.

Since 1974 the IEA has helped to create a world-wide network of 100 similar institutions in over 70 countries. They are all independent but share the IEA's mission.

Views expressed in the IEA's publications are those of the authors, not those of the Institute (which has no corporate view), its Managing Trustees, Academic Advisory Council members or senior staff.

Members of the Institute's Academic Advisory Council, Honorary Fellows, Trustees and Staff are listed on the following page.

The Institute gratefully acknowledges financial support for its publications programme and other work from a generous benefaction by the late Alec and Beryl Warren.

The Institute of Economic Affairs
2 Lord North Street, Westminster, London SW1P 3LB
Tel: 020 7799 8900
Fax: 020 7799 2137
Email: iea@iea.org.uk
Internet: iea.org.uk

Other papers recently published by the IEA include:

WHO, What and Why?

Transnational Government, Legitimacy and the World Health Organization
Roger Scruton
Occasional Paper 113; ISBN 0 255 36487 3
£8.00

The World Turned Rightside Up

A New Trading Agenda for the Age of Globalisation
John C. Hulsman
Occasional Paper 114; ISBN 0 255 36495 4
£8.00

The Representation of Business in English Literature

Introduced and edited by Arthur Pollard
Readings 53; ISBN 0 255 36491 1
£12.00

Anti-Liberalism 2000

The Rise of New Millennium Collectivism
David Henderson
Occasional Paper 115; ISBN 0 255 36497 0
£7.50

Capitalism, Morality and Markets
Brian Griffiths, Robert A. Sirico, Norman Barry & Frank Field
Readings 54; ISBN 0 255 36496 2
£7.50

A Conversation with Harris and Seldon
Ralph Harris & Arthur Seldon
Occasional Paper 116; ISBN 0 255 36498 9
£7.50

Malaria and the DDT Story
Richard Tren & Roger Bate
Occasional Paper 117; ISBN 0 255 36499 7
£10.00

A Plea to Economists Who Favour Liberty: Assist the Everyman
Daniel B. Klein
Occasional Paper 118; ISBN 0 255 36501 2
£10.00

The Changing Fortunes of Economic Liberalism
Yesterday, Today and Tomorrow
David Henderson
Occasional Paper 105 (new edition); ISBN 0 255 36520 9
£12.50

The Global Education Industry

Lessons from Private Education in Developing Countries
James Tooley
Hobart Paper 141 (new edition); ISBN 0 255 36503 9
£12.50

Saving Our Streams

*The Role of the Anglers' Conservation Association in
Protecting English and Welsh Rivers*
Roger Bate
Research Monograph 53; ISBN 0 255 36494 6
£10.00

Better Off Out?

The Benefits or Costs of EU Membership
Brian Hindley & Martin Howe
Occasional Paper 99 (new edition); ISBN 0 255 36502 0
£10.00

Buckingham at 25

Freeing the Universities from State Control
Edited by James Tooley
Readings 55; ISBN 0 255 36512 8
£15.00

Lectures on Regulatory and Competition Policy
Irwin M. Stelzer
Occasional Paper 120; ISBN 0 255 36511 X
£12.50

Misguided Virtue
False Notions of Corporate Social Responsibility
David Henderson
Hobart Paper 142; ISBN 0 255 36510 1
£12.50

HIV and Aids in Schools
The Political Economy of Pressure Groups and Miseducation
Barrie Craven, Pauline Dixon, Gordon Stewart & James Tooley
Occasional Paper 121; ISBN 0 255 36522 5
£10.00

The Road to Serfdom
The Reader's Digest *condensed version*
Friedrich A. Hayek
Occasional Paper 122; ISBN 0 255 36530 6
£7.50

Bastiat's *The Law*
Introduction by Norman Barry
Occasional Paper 123; ISBN 0 255 36509 8
£7.50

A Globalist Manifesto for Public Policy
Charles Calomiris
Occasional Paper 124; ISBN 0 255 36525 X
£7.50

Euthanasia for Death Duties
Putting Inheritance Tax Out of Its Misery
Barry Bracewell-Milnes
Research Monograph 54; ISBN 0 255 36513 6
£10.00

Liberating the Land
The Case for Private Land-use Planning
Mark Pennington
Hobart Paper 143; ISBN 0 255 36508 X
£10.00

IEA Yearbook of Government Performance 2002/2003
Edited by Peter Warburton
Yearbook 1; ISBN 0 255 36532 2
£15.00

Britain's Relative Economic Performance, 1870–1999
Nicholas Crafts
Research Monograph 55; ISBN 0 255 36524 1
£10.00

Should We Have Faith in Central Banks?
Otmar Issing
Occasional Paper 125; ISBN 0 255 36528 4
£7.50

The Dilemma of Democracy
Arthur Seldon
Hobart Paper 136 (reissue); ISBN 0 255 36536 5
£10.00

Capital Controls: a 'Cure' Worse Than the Problem?
Forrest Capie
Research Monograph 56; ISBN 0 255 36506 3
£10.00

The Poverty of 'Development Economics'
Deepak Lal
Hobart Paper 144 (reissue); ISBN 0 255 36519 5
£15.00

Should Britain Join the Euro?
The Chancellor's Five Tests Examined
Patrick Minford
Occasional Paper 126; ISBN 0 255 36527 6
£7.50

Post-Communist Transition: Some Lessons
Leszek Balcerowicz
Occasional Paper 127; ISBN 0 255 36533 0
£7.50

A Tribute to Peter Bauer
John Blundell et al.
Occasional Paper 128; ISBN 0 255 36531 4
£10.00

Employment Tribunals
Their Growth and the Case for Radical Reform
J. R. Shackleton
Hobart Paper 145; ISBN 0 255 36515 2
£10.00

Fifty Economic Fallacies Exposed
Geoffrey E. Wood
Occasional Paper 129; ISBN 0 255 36518 7
£12.50

A Market in Airport Slots
Keith Boyfield (editor), David Starkie, Tom Bass & Barry Humphreys
Readings 56; ISBN 0 255 36505 5
£10.00

Money, Inflation and the Constitutional Position of the Central Bank
Milton Friedman & Charles A. E. Goodhart
Readings 57; ISBN 0 255 36538 1
£10.00

railway.com
Parallels between the Early British Railways and the ICT Revolution
Robert C. B. Miller
Research Monograph 57; ISBN 0 255 36534 9
£12.50

The Regulation of Financial Markets
Edited by Philip Booth & David Currie
Readings 58; ISBN 0 255 36551 9
£12.50

Climate Alarmism Reconsidered

Robert L. Bradley Jr
Hobart Paper 146; ISBN 0 255 36541 1
£12.50

Government Failure: E. G. West on Education

Edited by James Tooley & James Stanfield
Occasional Paper 130; ISBN 0 255 36552 7
£12.50

Waging the War of Ideas

John Blundell
Second edition
Occasional Paper 131; ISBN 0 255 36547 0
£12.50

Corporate Governance: Accountability in the Marketplace

Elaine Sternberg
Second edition
Hobart Paper 147; ISBN 0 255 36542 X
£12.50

The Land Use Planning System
Evaluating Options for Reform
John Corkindale
Hobart Paper 148; ISBN 0 255 36550 0
£10.00

Economy and Virtue
Essays on the Theme of Markets and Morality
Edited by Dennis O'Keeffe
Readings 59; ISBN 0 255 36504 7
£12.50

Free Markets Under Siege
Cartels, Politics and Social Welfare
Richard A. Epstein
Occasional Paper 132; ISBN 0 255 36553 5
£10.00

Unshackling Accountants
D. R. Myddelton
Hobart Paper 149; ISBN 0 255 36559 4
£12.50

The Euro as Politics
Pedro Schwartz
Research Monograph 58; ISBN 0 255 36535 7
£12.50

Pricing Our Roads

Vision and Reality
Stephen Glaister & Daniel J. Graham
Research Monograph 59; ISBN 0 255 36562 4
£10.00

The Role of Business in the Modern World

Progress, Pressures, and Prospects for the Market Economy
David Henderson
Hobart Paper 150; ISBN 0 255 36548 9
£12.50

Public Service Broadcasting Without the BBC?

Alan Peacock
Occasional Paper 133; ISBN 0 255 36565 9
£10.00

The ECB and the Euro: the First Five Years

Otmar Issing
Occasional Paper 134; ISBN 0 255 36555 1
£10.00

Towards a Liberal Utopia?

Edited by Philip Booth
Hobart Paperback 32; ISBN 0 255 36563 2
£15.00

The Way Out of the Pensions Quagmire

Philip Booth & Deborah Cooper

Research Monograph 60; ISBN 0 255 36517 9

£12.50

Black Wednesday

A Re-examination of Britain's Experience in the Exchange Rate Mechanism

Alan Budd

Occasional Paper 135; ISBN 0 255 36566 7

£7.50

Crime: Economic Incentives and Social Networks

Paul Ormerod

Hobart Paper 151; ISBN 0 255 36554 3

£10.00

To order copies of currently available IEA papers, or to enquire about availability, please contact:

Lavis Marketing
IEA orders
FREEPOST LON21280
Oxford OX3 7BR

Tel: 01865 767575
Fax: 01865 750079
Email: orders@lavismarketing.co.uk

The IEA also offers a subscription service to its publications. For a single annual payment, currently £40.00 in the UK, you will receive every title the IEA publishes during the course of a year, invitations to events, and discounts on our extensive back catalogue. For more information, please contact:

Adam Myers
Subscriptions
The Institute of Economic Affairs
2 Lord North Street
London SW1P 3LB

Tel: 020 7799 8920
Fax: 020 7799 2137
Website: www.iea.org.uk